VISIONS of SOUTHWARK

V I S I O N S

o f

S O U T H W A R K

A COLLECTION OF NINETEENTH AND TWENTIETH
CENTURY PICTURE MATERIAL, PHOTOGRAPHS BY
LESLEY McDONALD, HISTORICAL NOTES, AND
DESCRIPTIVE, IMAGINATIVE WRITING

compiled and written
by
Peter Marcan

LONDON:
PETER MARCAN PUBLICATIONS
1997

© Peter Marcan, 1997.

Published by:
Peter Marcan Publications
PO Box 3158, London SE1 4RA
England, U.K. *Tel*: (0171) 357 0368

ISBN: 1 871811 13 9

COVER AND FRONTISPIECE

Front cover: Drawing by David Fried, 1996, of Borough High Street, looking north towards St George the Martyr Church, with Guy's Tower in the background.
Back cover: Etching 'Hop Exchange after fire', by Stanley Anderson, 1923.
Frontispiece: 'Prayer for my father', 1980's, by Jessica Wilkes.

ACKNOWLEDGEMENTS

The photographs of points of architectural and artistic interest and of buildings, were commissioned from Lesley McDonald who holds their copyright.
I am grateful to the following living artists who have given me permission to reproduce their work, and who own its copyright:
Frances Broomfield, Mike Challenger, Yolanda Christian, David Fried, Olwen Jones, Rod Judkins, George Large, Stephen Mumberson, Jen Parker, Hilary Paynter, Stan Peskett, David Tebbs, Sarah van Niekerk, Jessica Wilkes, Joseph Winkelman, and Ron Woollacott.
I am grateful to the following, acting on behalf of deceased artists, who have authorised reproduction of work:
Mrs Betty Anderson (for etching by Stanley Anderson), Marian Janes (for work by Norman Janes), the executors of the estate of Rachel Reckitt, Mrs Edna Williams (for work by Hubert Williams).
It has not proved possible to trace the next of kin/executors for: A.J. Laird, Frank Medworth, J. Paramor, David T. Rose (work held by the South London Gallery).
Nor has it proved possible (despite many enquiries) to trace the executor or next of kin for the estate of Hanslip Fletcher.
Any persons connected with the above deceased artists and to whom any reproduction fees may be due should not hesitate to contact the compiler/publisher.
Lastly, thanks to staff at Southwark Local Studies Library, and to the various organisations who supplied information.

Printed and bound by SRP, Exeter.

CONTENTS

LONDON BRIDGE FANTASIA

Do not try to understand what this crazy turmoil of a place is all about, as it is quite beyond all understanding. Point of arrival and departure, human society here is so chaotic, so entangled, all on the move, that no one can surely make head or tail of it at all.

During office hours faces gaze out of a hundred and one office windows, fists long to smash into smithereens a hundred and one computer screens; caged in during office hours, the home going time is a stampede of people who have become like animals in a zoo let loose. At home going time it is frightening to behold the savage desperation of so many people on their way out; do not scrutinise these people too closely: the young men may give you a karate chop in the stomach, the young women will cut you down with withering glances.

You hear the music of Bela Bartok in this place: everything out of synchrony, jangling dissonance and frenzied inner despair; shrieking stumps of humanity, bodies lurching forward, minds crushed into nothingness.

"Promise me you will practise your Bartok", said the artist Mike Challenger when I visited him at his studio home in Park Street; and after our meeting when he played Bach preludes and fugues to me, we went out and heard the squeals of incoming and outgoing trains, felt the abandonment of the market emptied of its traders, yet still full of intangible energy, and saw the desperate gregariousness of people away from their work pouring drink down through their throats in street corner pubs.

Above: *London Bridge Station*, wood engraving by Rachel Reckitt, from *London South of the River* by Sam Price Myers, published by Paul Elek in 1949. A striking evocation of the station's manic mood at night-time.

Above: *The hop-pickers' exodus: London Bridge Station at midnight*; from the London Argus, September 3, 1897. An earlier depiction of the same subject, also with figures smoking, by Enoch Ward, appeared in Black and White, 1892.

3

Above: A drawing by David Fried, 1996, suggesting that 145 years from the illustration below, something has gone horribly wrong in society: a group of disorientated, terrified individuals have arrived at their destination: they do not connect with one another, have identity confusion, and may be close to real madness. The station, rebuilt in the late 1970's by British Rail's architects department, has we note lost its 'B'.

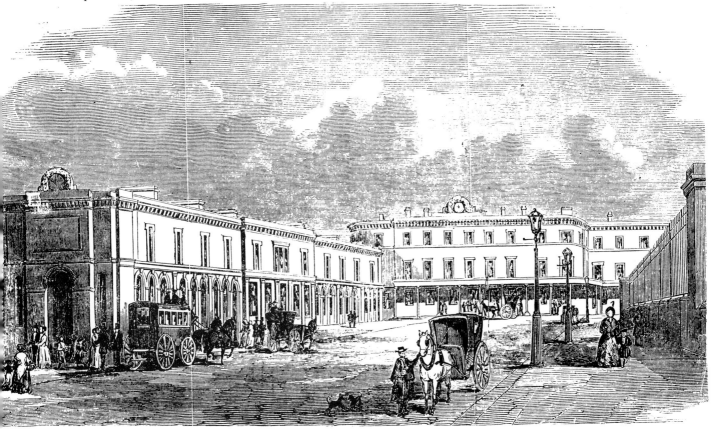

bove: *The new terminus of the South-Eastern Railway, at London Bridge,* from the Illustrated London News, February 15, 1851. ondon Bridge Station opened in 1836. The first 'proper' station buildings were erected 1840-44 (see illustration in Illustrated ndon News, February 3, 1844), and later rebuilt in 1849 by Samuel Beazley. The above scene is a touching view of intimate ationships. An article 'A day at London Bridge Station' appeared in the Illustrated London News, July 24, 1858.

Above: *London Bridge Station and Southwark Cathedral, 1930's*: gouache painting by David T. Rose. Courtesy: South London Art Gallery. Rain, taxis, a porter, the cathedral in the background: a daytime scene of normality.

Above: *Interior of the AB signal box at London Bridge Railway Station*; from the Penny Illustrated Magazine, 17 July, 1868; (an exterior view is also depicted).

Above: *London Bridge Railway Terminus Hotel*; from the Illustrated London News, August 3, 1861. The hotel stood just behind the eighteenth century part of St Thomas' Hospital; built in 1861, architect: Henry Currey, it had some 150 rooms. It apparently attracted little custom and was purchased by the London, Brighton and South Coast Railway Board in 1893 and used for offices and then demolished in 1941. Besant's *London South of the Thames* reproduces a painting of the building and Southwark Local Studies has a framed coloured lithograph of the interior by Robert Dudley.

Above: *A view of the approach to London Bridge, 1830's*. Courtesy: Southwark Local Studies Library. The Ash printing building has been replaced with Bank Chambers.

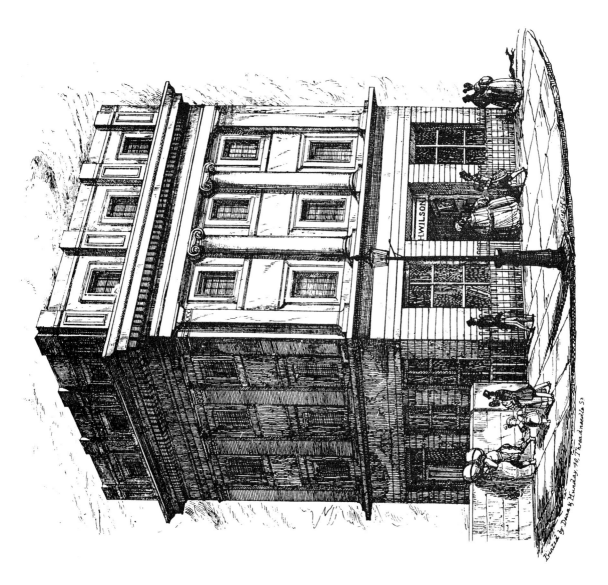

Above: *Henry Wilson's tea, grocery, and spice warehouse, at number one, Wellington Street, London Bridge.* A nineteenth century trade publicity sheet. The uppermost part of Borough High Street was once known as Wellington Street. The building shown later became Bridge House Hotel. It was erected by the Hays Wharf Company, 1834, architect: George Allen, and ceased as a hotel in the mid 1960's.

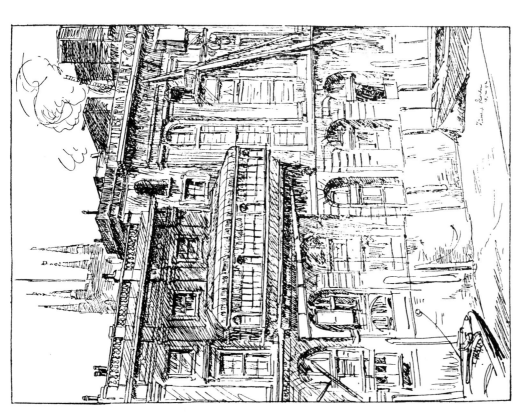

Above: A drawing by Hanslip Fletcher, from the Pall Mall Magazine, March 8, 1912, showing *Hibernia Chambers*, 1850, and warehouse, 1808, below. Hibernia Wharf has now been replaced with an office block. The Worshipful Companies of Glaziers and Painters of Glass, of Scientific Instrument Makers, and of Launderers have offices here (entrance in Montague Place).

Above: *Old London Bridge from Southwark, showing the bridge after its alterations 1758-62*; a print, c. 1830 by W. Radcliffe after a drawing by T.H. Shepherd.

Opposite: A painting, 1990's by Frances Broomfield, inspired by the poem *After London*, by J.D.C. Pellow, and based around a Museum of London model and various illustrations. The interest focuses, however, on the foreground scene, and the sense that with the demise of London untamed nature will quickly return.

Peter de Colechurch's bridge was built between 1176 and 1209 and survived for over 600 years.

Below: *New London Bridge, with the Lord Mayor's procession passing under the unfinished arches*, November 9, 1827; drawn by T.H. Shepherd, engraved by T. Higham, 1828. The new bridge opened in 1831, replaced in its turn by today's 1973 bridge.

Above: *Charing Cross Railway* – work in progress on the line leading out of London Bridge Station; from the Illustrated London News, February 7, 1863. The iron girder bridge is shown nearing completion in a later engraving in the Illustrated London News, October 1863. St Thomas' Hospital was a casualty of this enterprise, and is shown on the far left: on the far

UP AND DOWN IN BOROUGH HIGH STREET

It is hard to make much sense of Borough High Street today, a street so historical, but with nothing much left of its prisons and inns for which it was once famous; the jagged roof line, the small, tall buildings, the small courts and turnings leading off on both sides of the road just hinting at its long-gone medieval past. Today, with only a few years left before the Millennium, the street often seems totally mad by day, desolate and numbing in its dullness in the evenings. Countless people come down to the topmost end from all over to reach Guy's Hospital; tourists come here, drawn here by Southwark Cathedral and the George Inn. You might see them with their guide books peering down the little courtyards, wondering themselves quite what they are seeking.

Only one side of the George Inn survives, its rebuilding dates from after the 1676 Southwark fire. Taken over by the National Trust in 1937, and leased to Whitbreads, the interior rooms contain a variety of old prints and photographs; tucked away in the atmospheric 'old bar' on the right as you enter the courtyard you will find two strange, murky prints by R.A. Webb dated 1989 and 1990. A golden bell hangs over the National Trust Plaque and there are hanging baskets at all three levels. In the ugly, modern construction to the north and east a wine bar the Guinea Butt and the Alianti Sandwich Bar compete for custom. Three different pub signs depict St George, and lastly you may notice the commendation 'Evening Standard 1995 Pub of the Year' on the entrance gate. Another green dragon, much longer and headless, coils round part of the wall of the tunnel under London Bridge – a new restaurant Dragon's Lair is here.

In King's Head Yard we find the Kind's Head Pub, 1881, with a colourful bust of Henry VIII perched high up, and in Newcomen Street the Kings Arms Pub, 1890, with its eighteenth century arms taken from the gatehouse of London Bridge when remodelled 1758-62. On the corner of Chapel Court further down the street is the four-storeyed Blue Eyed Maid, with an attractive sign and decorative brickwork.

Walking up and down this street on many occasions, a local person may conclude that this is a street given over wholly to the business of making money, that no one loves this street. Walking up from Borough underground station, the sprawling Brandon House seems remote in time and spirit from the palace of Charles Brandon, Duke of Suffolk once here. Behind lies Little Dorrit Park; from here the spire of St George the Martyr stares out balefully and questioningly, seems to be reminding us that the shrubbery and trees by the wall are stronger forces than the brickwork and clever machines in the building behind. Offices and more offices to let are around here: empty, impersonal places no one loves. For some years an international human rights organisation Article 19 was at number 90, bringing a mood of dissent to the place, but now it has gone from here. Founded by Kevin Boyle, Article 19 was here from 1986-94 and is in Islington today. Some courtyards around here look vaguely intriguing: Henry Gross Ltd, importers and distributors of basket and caneware have been at Maidstone Buildings for some 40 years; the firm was founded in 1901, and the managing director mentioned to me their uncertain future here with property developers often on the warpath. Offices are situated in Calverts Buildings, timber framed, with over-hanging upper floor; adjacent are the premises of Field & Son, estate agents and surveyors since 1803. Their building at number 54 dates back to the mid-sixteenth century, and with the firm wanting to move out there are plans to turn it into a Dickens museum (Southwark News, July 18th, 1996).

Perambulating the eastern side of the street, one will find dentists and newsagents, and a diversity of other commercial places. The shelves at the newsagents are filled to overflowing with all the latest magazine titles: all the latest obsessions and specialist interests are transformed into glossy graphic art, screaming out their messages.

Close to the George Inn at number 67 is the late nineteenth century building of W.H. Lemay, hop factors, with an attractive carved panel showing hop gathering. Large stores were once here too: at number 161 is Albion House, former premises of the clothing firm Gainsford & Co founded in 1819, and now occupied by the Tile Centre. We are now well off the tourist beaten track, back into the agony of the late twentieth century: students at Accountancy Tutors Ltd and the University of Humberside School of Finance and Management puff at their cigarettes and scrutinise one another for clues of their future, at numbers 179-191. Local government offices pursue their bureaucratic tasks with diligence in Angel Court and at 215-221 the Chartered Institute of Public Finance and Accountancy has an education and training centre.

Above: 'The Borough', near London Bridge Railway Station; from a price list of c. 1865 of Newsom & Co, tea merchants; an evocative depiction of the northern most end of Borough High Street, and a variety of horse driven vehicles; Duke Street Hill, Railway Approach, and London Bridge Street are the three turnings shown. Courtesy: Southwark Local Studies Library.

© DAVID FRIED 1996

Opposite: *The St Saviour's parish World War I memorial* at the northern end of Borough High Street, in front of Town Hall Chambers (plaque on right-hand side). Unveiled in 1922, the work was sculpted by P. Lindsey Clerk (1889-1977). Another work of his, in similar style, is The Cameronians (Scottish Rifles) memorial, located near Glasgow Art Gallery, Kelvingrove Park. The relief carvings on the pedestal depict military scenes, mother and child and St George and dragon.

To the north we see New London Bridge House, and the entrance to the George Inn between Lloyds Bank and George House.

Opposite: *Queen's Head Inn*; from the Illustrated London News, February 26, 1887. Owned in the seventeenth century by John Harvard's father, a borough High Street butcher. The site is recorded on a plaque at the offices of B.M. Birnberg & Co, 103 Borough High Street (John Harvard House). The patiently waiting horse, and the two small groups give the scene a sense of lassitude and finality, before a building shuts down.

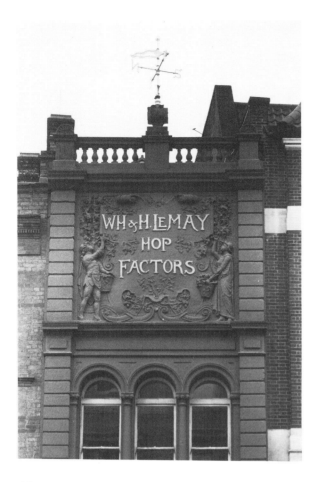

Above: This decorative panel, preserved as a record of an industry which has now left the area, is close to the Southwark Street junction, and may have been inspired by the relief carving over the old Hop Exchange; the facade is inspired, perhaps, by the old town hall building.

Above: *The Town Hall, Borough, just demolished*; from the Illustrated London News, November 26th, 1859. This second town hall was erected in 1793, replacing the 1686 building (see the reproduction of the Wilkinson print). There is a water-colour by T.H. Shepherd, c. 1828, engraved by R. Winkles. The Victorian building Town Hall Chambers stands on the site.

Above: *Old houses in Borough High Street*; a drawing by Hubert Williams, 1920's. Courtesy: Southwark Local Studies Library.

Above: *New City and South London Railway*: station in the Borough; from an article in the Illustrated London News, November 8, 1890 on the opening of the new line extending to Stockwell. Kennington Station still has its original domed lift structure.

Above: *View of the Town Hall, St Margaret's Hill, Southwark, previous to the present erection by the Corporation of London, in 1793*; drawn by Ravenhill, engraved by Thomas Dale, and published by Robert Wilkinson, 1825; courtesy: Southwark Local Studies Library. The artist takes delight in an early morning, sunlit scene, birds soaring and only a few locals about who do not disturb the view.

Opposite: Interior view of the (
Inn; a wood engraving by Rachel f
published in *London South of the*
1949.

We guess that some kind of deal is
to be made, and sense that the b
will be all ears for both sides
negotiation. The chair ruminates
never-ending roundabout of life.

Above and opposite: Two drawings from an article *At a
famous Southwark hotel*, published in the London Argus,
March 1, 1901.

The scene above suggests a cold winter's morning. In the
coffee room, opposite, newspapers are spread out, and the
table is laid out for the first customers.

Above: An engraving from *White & Co's 1852 Almanack*, issued 'gratis, with the view to give respectable and increased publicity to their tea establishment'. Courtesy: Southwark Local Studies Library.

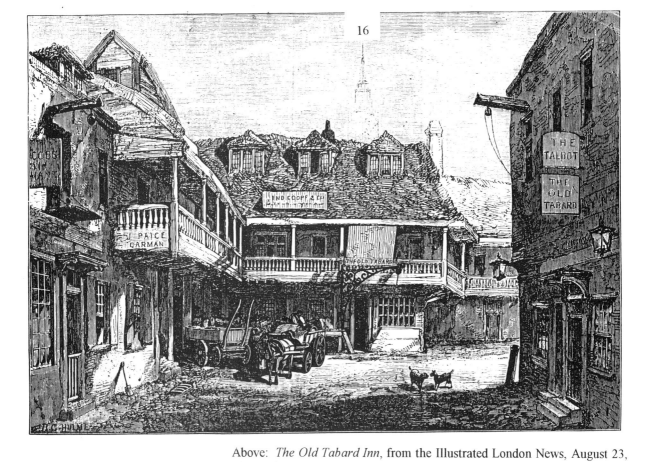

Above: *The Old Tabard Inn*, from the Illustrated London News, August 23, 1873. The scene shows the inn shortly before its demolition, in use for storage. It was known as the Tabard (a knight's sleeveless jacket) in Chaucer's time, but after rebuilding, after the 1676 fire, was renamed the Talbot (a white hunting hound). Talbot Yard records the site. There is an etching, 1875 by Percy Thomas.

Opposite: A pencil drawing, 1936, by Joan Blo
courtesy:
London Borough of Lambeth Archives Departmen

Above: *The White Hart Inn*: from the Builder, October 14, 1865. The inn dates back to the fifteenth century; it was partially rebuilt after the 1669 fire, and demolished in 1889; it is commemorated by White Hart Yard. Southwark Local Studies Library has some interesting photographs of the 1880's showing a run-down building, prior to demolition, and an etching, 1882 by Percy Thomas (Whistler's first pupil), (reproduced in SB & R in Old Photographs).

Above: *The Catherine Wheel*; from Once a Week, January 26, 1867.

Above: *Sign of the Blue Eyed Maid pub* at 173 Borough High Street.

Above: An engraving from the cover of a sales catalogue 'List of cheap winter goods', of one of Southwark's old big stores, established in 1819, and located at 161-167 Borough High Street. Courtesy: Southwark Local Studies Library. On the wall you can still read: 'The monster ready made and bespoke clothing establishment; branch establishments in Paris, Antwerp, Ghent'.

Above: *The Palace of Southwark*: an engraving from the Illustrated London News, March 24, 1860, based on The View of London, c. 1543 by Anthony de Wyngaerde. He came to England in 1541 and made drawings of buildings. The Duke of Suffolk's palace was taken over by Henry VIII and used as a mint. The building later passed to Nicholas Heath, Archbishop of York who sold the property which was then dismantled. The remaining property passed to John Broomfield, son of a Lord Mayor, who married the daughter of a merchant Thomas Lant, who developed the estate in the eighteenth century. The Lant family sold the property in 1811.

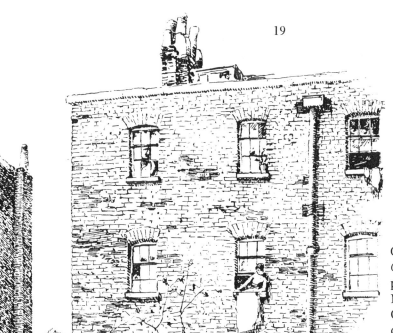

Opposite: *The Marshalsea – from St George's Churchyard*; a drawing by A.D. M'Cormick, published in the English Illustrated Magazine, November, 1888.

Other depictions of the prison at the time of its demolition include: water-colour, 1887, by John Crowther (in Guildhall Library); and illustration in the Graphic, January 1887. Earlier water-colours (in Guildhall Library) include a view of the wall, 1877 (reproduced in 'Charles Dickens and Southwark'), and a view of the keeper's house, 1832 (reproduced in SB & R in Old Photographs).

The prison stood for many centuries on a site at Mermaid Court; the name is derived from the Marshal of the King's household. It was an important prison under Elizabeth I, not only for debtors, but for anyone thought to be defying authority. It moved to a site just north of St George's church at the end of the 18th century and closed in 1842. Dicken's father was imprisoned here for debt in 1824.

Below: *North view of the Marshalsea, Southwark, before the new buildings*; an engraving 'by T.P., after a drawing by Orme', late eighteenth century. Courtesy: London Borough of Lambeth Archives Department. Another view (showing the seventeenth century court house) was engraved by I. Lewis in 1773, and issued by Robert Wilkinson in 1812 (with key to identify parts), reproduced in SB & R in Old Photographs, and Survey of London, Vol XXV.

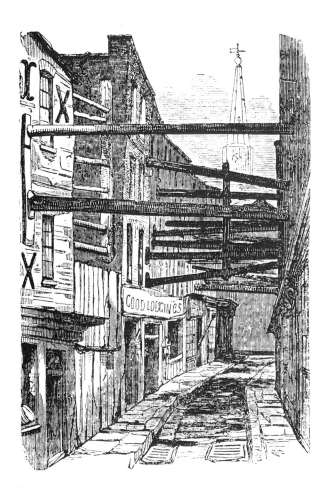

The Builder investigates poverty in nineteenth century Southwark:

Above: *Ewer Street, Gravel Lane.* A location known as James' Place is shown. Gravel Lane was the upper part of Great Suffolk Street.

Above: *Mint Street, looking towards High Street.*

Bottom: *Duke Street* (today Duke Street Hill, Tooley Street). The above are from the Builder, November 5, 1853.

Centre: *May-pole Alley* (site of Maypole House). From the Builder, September 16, 1865.

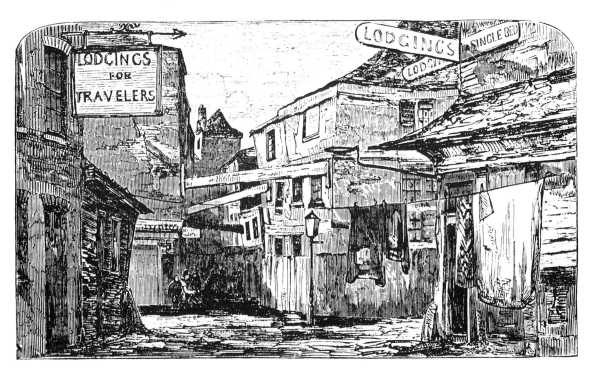

Above: From a trade leaflet, early nineteenth century, advertising the firm's mourning dress services. The second St George the Martyr church was erected in 1736, architect: John Prince; the ceiling was designed in 1897 by Basil Champneys. The modern eastern window by Marion Grant shows the Ascension, with Little Dorrit kneeling.

Above: *Steps leading from the church to the crypt*: a drawing from an illustrated article 'The crypt of Little Dorrit's church', Daily Graphic, March 28, 1906. Courtesy: Southwark Local Studies Library.

bove and opposite right: Drawings by l Prince from article 'Relics of ckens', by Charles W. Dickens, unsey's Magazine, September 1902. pposite, left: A drawing by A.D. Cormick of the vestry from article harles Dickens in London', English ustrated Magazine, November 1888.

© DAVID FRIED 1996

Above: A drawing by David Fried, 1996, showing the tunnel approach to *Green Dragon Court*, and girders of railway bridge above, at northern end of Borough High Street. As in his other drawings, the artist lavishes attention on a somewhat bizarre landscape, whilst also commenting on individuals' ability to survive in it: a solitary figure consults his notes, whilst an embracing couple saunter away quite unconcerned. The name of the courtyard area is a reference to an inn here: St Saviour's Grammar School was also here from 1562 to 1838.

HOSPITAL LAND: Guy's Hospital, and St Thomas Street

This is the land of dread and death, of desire and desperation: this is the land of the medics.

Medical students clutch their overtaxed brains, brains they feel are bursting out of their skulls, such are the demands of their five year long studies; driven on by a desire for professional status, whipped on by their teachers, peers and parents, they can work themselves into exhaustion, until they collapse on their beds late at night and at once are snoring blissfully.

Visitors to patients in the hospital are full of trepidation and desperation, not knowing whether their loved ones will manage to pull through. They come by train from all parts of the country: they leave with anguish, relief, sadness, or joy.

Doctors are faced with impossible dilemmas, are driven almost to breaking point with overwork; are conscious of their rivals and colleagues, feel driven to establish or reinforce professional reputations.

Yet, if you come here on Sundays, bank holidays, or Easter or Christmas Day (as you wend your way to the Cathedral), the mood of anguish has dissolved, and everything is silent and still. You can wander around the courtyards of the eighteenth century building and see no one; see no one, yet sense that you are in a venerable and prestigious place, cherished by those departed and now in practice in all corners of the world, and students arriving here for the first time sense they have joined a distinguished and elitist kind of place.

This is a place which is aware of the contributions made by individuals to society and wishes to honour them. There are two statues to Thomas Guy (1664-1724): one by Peter Scheemakers (famous for his statue to Shakespeare in Westminster Abbey), 1734 in the forecourt, showing Thomas Guy distinguished, yet humble, with religious reliefs on two sides of the pedestal; another in the chapel to the right, by John Bacon (represented in Westminster Abbey by his memorial to Lord Chatham), 1779, depicts Thomas Guy welcoming a sick person into his hospital. There is a statue to Lord Nuffield, 1949, by Maurice Lambert (1902-64, brother of composer Constant Lambert) in the courtyard to the right of the central colonnade. Lord Nuffield funded Nuffield House, a private wing of the hospital. There are also memorial plaques and tablets: to Frederick Pedley who founded the Dental School in 1889, in the central colonnade; a memorial to victims of war in South Africa, 1899-1902 in the courtyard to the left, and a large World War II memorial arch at the southern end of the park, represented here in 1994.

The windows in the chapel, depicting biblical scenes of healing commemorate William Hunt, a wealthy merchant and benefactor to the hospital, also buried with Thomas Guy in the chapel, and also remembered at Hunt's House, the Victorial block, 1852, with northern wing of 1871, to the east of the park. Indeed the chapel commemorates many people: governors, benefactors, and matrons. To the right by the entrance there is an impressive memorial to William Withey Gull, 1816-90, physician to Queen Victoria, lecturer and governor at the hospital; in the gallery upstairs one will find plaques to Thomas Addison, and Sir William Arbutnot Lane.

Over the entrance gate (the railings date from 1741) in St Thomas Street, there for all to ponder on, are the words of Thomas Guy's motto: dare quam accipere, (to give, rather than to receive). As the students drop off to sleep after another hard day, do they find themselves mumbling these words of comfort: dare quam accipere, dare quam accipere?

EPILOGUE:

It is best not to linger in hospital land, with all its pain, and anguish and the agony of its terminal cases and the profound anxiety of the next of kin. It is much better to move away from all this, to turn one's back on it all with immense, if anguished disdain, and move away towards Bermondsey Street and sit in the rose garden, off Morocco Street, be amused by the new block Leathermarket Court, with its slender, segmented pillars, and little left hand side wing), to gaze into the blue skies, full of ebullient clouds, aeroplanes soaring through them on their way to foreign lands, leaving behind, down below, an agonised nation, full of perplexed and troubled individuals, straying around demented with foreboding and grief.

A Guy's medical student writes ...

Walking through the gates of Guy's Hospital as a student for the first time will probably be the most memorable occurrence of my life. The feeling was one of sheer exultation. After many years of strenuous endeavour, passing innumerable exams and surviving gruelling interviews, I had not only been rewarded with the realisation of my life-long ambition to read medicine, but also honoured, by being admitted to the medical school associated with arguably the two most prestigious and well-known hospitals in the world.

Even after spending three fruitful years here, each time I stroll through Memorial Park at Guy's, the aura exuded by the place never fails to overawe me. It has a unique liveliness, a hustle and bustle, a sense of warmth that is borne out by the intriguingly complex mix of its famous physicians, renowned teachers, hospital staff, researchers, and patients. The essence of all this, of course, is the illustrious history and the tradition. What a privilege it is to be clerking on the same wards that luminaries such as Gull, Hopkins and Babington once graced, or pacing corridors that were the domain of Astley Cooper, Aston Key and Hilton. How often have I marvelled at specimens in the museums that were donated by none other than Addison, Bright and Hodgkin, and meandered through colonnades and old lecture theatres that were frequented by Keats! What would these dignitaries have thought of the modern hospital and the latest in medical technology or of an ambulance tearing through Bermondsey with its lights flashing and siren wailing, an incident which I witness daily? What would they think of teaching and students today as opposed to the patriarchal system of apprenticeships? On a lighter note, one thing is for certain. Lectures are still as fatuous in 1997, as they were in 1815 and I wholly sympathise with Keats when he wrote "the other day during the lecture there came a sunbeam into the room, and with it a whole troop of creatures floating in the ray, and I was off with them to Oberon and fairyland"!

Today, Guy's Hospital is still seen as the pinnacle of medical care and the Medical School is very progressive in its outlook. Its pupils come from all over the globe, many of whom subsequently rise to celebrity and hold offices and appointments elsewhere. On campus, however, this diverse student body shares together the emotions of the toils of life in London. Similarly, patients also represent a host of nationalities and are admitted from as far afield as Alaska or Australia. No longer is a distinction between the affluent and the pauper made or between the treatable and incurable, as it used to be: care in this epoch is available to everyone who needs it.

As a student and one of its would-be doctors, I have always advocated Guy's motto of *Dare Quam Accipere* and would implore all others who will inevitably become bonded to this great hospital to do the same. Their patrimony is second to none and they must uphold and promulgate shamelessly and forthrightly, its governing philanthropic ideals. So long as the tradition of loyal and unselfish service is maintained, the Medical School can face the future with optimism and aplomb, whilst looking back with just pride and contentment on the past.

Fraz A. Mir, December 1996

Above: *Opening the winter season at Guy's: the rush adjournment to the Bridge House Hotel*, London Bridge; from Pictorial World, October 17, 1874. The scene refers to an overcrowded lecture at the hospital which was transferred to the hotel.

Above: *Houses, Guy's Hospital*, from the Builder, September 12, 1863. This rather splendid, ornate building, architect: Newman & Billing, is now known as Keats House; it is owned by the Special Trustees of Guy's Hospital, and doctors have private consultancy rooms here. Keats, the poet, was a Guy's medical student. To the right is the 1980's office block New City Court and to the left Conybeare House (named after the physician and author Sir John Conybeare). Beyond lies the latest development Thomas Guy House, completed in 1996, architects: Watkins Gray International.

Above: A lino-cut by Stephen Mumberson, 1991, showing *Guy's Tower* as seen from London Bridge Station. The artist cleverly suggests the surgical activity of a hospital in his depiction of this thirty-storey block, built 1963-75, architects: Watkins Gray Woodgate International. It is the area's dominating landmark. The service tower on the left has a lecture theatre in the uppermost surgical instrument-like part.

Above: A drawing from *South London*, by Walter Besant, Chatto & Windus, 1901. The apartments of the treasurer of St Thomas' Hospital were here. The building is early eighteenth century, now known as Collegiate House and occupied by Butcher, Robinson and Staples group of companies.

Above: A drawing by Hubert Williams, 1920's, showing *old St Thomas' church*, built 1702-03 and adjacent terrace. Courtesy: Southwark Local Studies Library. The tower must be unique in housing an old operating theatre, built in 182 and rediscovered in 1956, and a 'herb garret', and now open to the public as a museum (guide book published in 1996) Poetry readings are also held there; the early nineteenth century terrace, Mary Sheridan House is occupied by the Lambeth, Southwark and Lewisham Health Authority.

Above: *New warehouses, St Thomas Street;* architect: Henry Currey (who also designed the London Bridge Terminus Hotel); from the Builder, March 20, 1875. Bevington's had their leather warehouse and office here at number 42 from 1875 until 1940, when bombed, close to other leather firms to the east of Guy's Hospital. A detailed account of the firm is given in *Bevington & Son, Bermondsey, 1795-1950, a chronicle* by Geoffrey Bevington, 1993.

Above and below, left: Two drawings from *Guy's Hospital, 1724-1902*, published by Ash & Co, 1903. *Hunt's House*, above, dates from 1851; the turrets were designed as ventilation ducts (see Illustrated London News October 9, 1852). The demolition of Hunt's House is imminent, to make way for the campus of the amalgamated medical schools of Guy's, St Thomas', and King's College. The roof-tops are of former clinical wards, now gone.

Below, left: *Balconies recently added to surgical wards with new isolation ward below*, (now gone).

Below, right: *Coat of arms of Thomas Guy over St Thomas Street main entrance.*

Above: *New medical residential college, Guy's Hospital*; from Pictorial World, April 13, 1890. This building stood just south of Hunt's House in Great Maze Pond. The site is now occupied by Guy's Tower; it was demolished in 1965-66 and replaced by Wolfson House, a hostel for medical students in Weston Street, 1977.

Above: The finely cast statue to *Thomas Guy* in the hospital front quadrangle.

Opposite: A drawing by Hubert Williams, 1931; courtesy: Southwark Local Studies Library. The alcove comes from the redesigned mid-eighteenth century London Bridge and has been in the courtyard to the left of the colonnade since 1926.

Opposite: *Southwark Tower, St Thomas Street*, completed 1975; UK and World Headquarters of Price Waterhouse, accountancy firm (the partnership dates back to 1865); a drawing by David Fried, 1996. Any comment on this powerful drawing must come from the reader's own imagination.

SOUTHWARK CATHEDRAL: Easter Day

Hemmed in by twentieth century commercialism, screeched at by incoming and outgoing trains, Southwark Cathedral is secure in its ancient plot beside London Bridge. One senses at once that it is still a dominant spiritual presence, indeed the very heart of the far reaching Diocese of Southwark, as lovingly depicted in a remarkable map drawn by Jen Parker and published in 1987 by Friends of Southwark Cathedral: churches and people spilling out throughout South London and down to Reigate and Godstone. A cathedral only since 1897, its full name, the Cathedral Church of St Saviour and St Mary Overie indicates its past: in Norman and medieval times the priory church of St Mary Overie, and from the sixteenth century the parish church of Saint Saviour. The pinnacled tower we see today dating from 1689, beckons to us with friendly charm; from the end of Borough High Street, from vantage points across the river, from neighbouring streets it hints strongly at the survival of belief amidst the centuries of clamour this historic place has known.

Alive, and flourishing, the cathedral is a haven for those weary after a long train journey, a point of pilgrimage for American tourists searching for memorials to bishops, playwrights, and philanthropists, a place for music recitals, concerts and special commemoration services.

I went there one Easter Day for the service at 11.00. I arrived in good time. Members of the congregation were handed candles. Vergers bobbed about with medallions on red ribbons around their necks. I looked at the crowd of people assembled. Where had they all come from, how had they got through their lives so far, where were they all in their different lives? I wondered. All this was impossible to know, but they looked blank, numb, emptied, so I thought. Awaiting the alleluias of resurrection, the faithful assembled here had come to praise the triumph of light over darkness, of warmth over coldness, of the beginning of new life, as the heavy stone of nihilism was turned aside by the angel of resurrection.

We all turned to face the bishop and his men of God as the Paschal candle finally spluttered into life and was borne aloft, a small, tiny fleck of a flame that persisted as it was carried down the aisle. Words of proclamation were uttered, a Schubert gloria came from the choir, hymns of praise were sung. The bishop mounted the pulpit and spoke of the symbolism of the stone at the tomb of Christ, of the triumph of God over the crushing meanness of sinful humanity. Then there was a baptism, a new child called Gregory Benedictus Jeremiah had come into the world, and the bishop told us how thrilled he was to find yet another Christian soul, so thrilled he could shout with joy. Then one by one came a procession of laity, bearing the silver vessels of communion; stepping along one by one, I thought they looked transfixed, stepping out from the distant past, engaging in rituals known to antiquity. Then came Easter eggs, and laughter; eggs for the choir boys, the children, even an egg for the manager of the cathedral bookshop. The choir processed back down the aisle of the nave, singing heartily. Glasses of sherry were being laid out on a long table; the men of God stood around in their white robes, saturated in scripture; what could I possibly speak to them of? I wondered.

I wandered out, a bit dazed, a bit numb, feeling of not much significance, out into the spring sunlight and walked back home to Bermondsey.

Above: *The chapel in the church of St Saviour, Southwark, in which are interred the remains of Dr Lancelot Andrews*; an engravin
by Dale of a drawing by Schnebbelie, published by Robert Wilkinson, 1825. Courtesy: Southwark Local Studies Library. The chap
was demolished in 1830 for road widening.

CATHEDRAL STIMULATION: Monuments and stained glass

Most cathedrals contain much to delight the eye and stimulate one's historical curiosity, if one is intent on seeking it out. As we enter Southwark Cathedral at the southern door, we may be overcome by the sweeping, yet somewhat austere vista of the nave (rebuilt in the 1890's), leading the eye forward to the high altar and Sir John Ninian Comper's 1951 window of Christ, the Virgin Mary, and St John the Evangelist.

We need, however, to linger at the western end, and ponder awhile on the grandeur and misery of existence, its ecstasy and futility, as expressed in memorials and artefacts around here. The Marchioness boat disaster of 1989 is recorded in a plaque on the floor, and we will pause to note the tragically youthful ages of the victims. The collection of carved wooden bosses from the nave's fifteenth century roof depict greedy, devouring faces and convoluted birds and animals; but towering over all this is the pre-Raphaelite style 'creation' window by Henry Holiday, 1903, the six days of creation represented in six circles. It is surmounted by carved musicians from the 1703 organ: David with harp and two trumpeting angels. Also at the western end is the block marble font with towering canopy, by G.F. Bodley.

Stained glass is often full of imagery and Kenneth London (in his book *Stained glass in Southwark Cathedral*) is right to urge readers to come with their binoculars. In the south aisle we will find twenty-four figures crowded into Christopher Webb's extraordinary Shakespeare memorial window of 1954: figures from the comedies and tragedies, with Prospero, Ariel and Caliban in the central light, and at the base, figures depicting the seven ages of man from *As you like it*. Below the window is the brown alabaster Shakespeare monument by Henry McCarthy, 1912, with a relief carving of seventeenth century Southwark behind.

Continuing eastwards into the retrochoir (behind the high altar) we will find the fascinating Rider window by Lawrence Lee, 1959. This commemorates the rebuilding of the nave in 1895 by Thomas Francis Rider's firm and depicts scenes from the building and rebuilding of the cathedral from the ninth century to the time of the nineteenth century restoration intertwined with twentieth century figures representing different building trades. The final scene depicts figures from different periods standing in prayer around the cathedral tower. The new nave is the work of Sir Arthur Bloomfield. George Gwilt, Junior was responsible for the restoration of the choir and tower, 1818-23, and the retrochoir in 1833. You find his tomb outside in the churchyard (the only one remaining) between the buttresses of the south choir aisle.

In the north aisle there are stained glass windows commemorating seven famous personalities connected with Southwark or the cathedral: Oliver Goldsmith, Samuel Johnson, Henry Sacheverall (1705-1790, controversial preacher and chaplain of St Saviour's), Alexander Cruden, John Bunyan, John Gower, and Geoffrey Chaucer. John Gower's richly ornate tomb lies below his window.

The cathedral's monuments are especially resplendent; not visible as we enter, they must be searched out in the transepts and the two choir aisles. We can gaze searchingly at these curious faces from the past, and discern perhaps a certain piety, mixed with a certain kind of humour. The early seventeenth century Humble and Trehearne memorials are especially appealing. John Trehearne's six offspring kneel below him in a charming carved relief. Alderman Richard Humble and his two wives kneel beneath a decorated canopy, their offspring likewise below. Nearby is the celebrated oaken effigy of a recumbent, cross-legged knight from about 1275 and close by an effigy of an emaciated corpse, which really seems more suited for a crypt. In the south choir aisle there are memorials to two ecclesiastical personalities of importance: the tomb of the great Bishop Lancelot Andrewes, the last bishop to live at Winchester House, with a modern canopy by Comper, and some antique notes and drawings for visitors. A selection of his prayers has been published recently by Friends of Southwark Cathedral. Beside him is the monument to Edward Talbot, the first Bishop of Southwark, 1905-11, designed by Cecil Thomas. We gaze at this long, robed figure, protected with eagles, lions, and two bibles open at his feet, and we know we are being asked to feel awe and respect.

We encounter less famous figures in the transepts: the allegorical Austin monument by Nicholas Stone, erected by lawyer William Austin in 1633 in memory of his mother, a benefactress of the church; the guilded angel of resurrection and the two resting haymakers with broad sun hats form an intimate, yet dramatic composition of some originality. There is the languid, reclining figure of Lionel Lockyer, a physician famous for his pills, 1672. In the south transept there is the curious, miniature death bed monument to William Emerson, 1575, founder of one of the parish charities; here we also find busts to John Bingham, 1625, a saddler to Elizabeth I and James I, and a vestryman, to Richard Benefield, mid seventeenth century, and beneath him, to Sir Frederick Wigan, cross-armed, treasurer and benefactor during the Victorian restoration period. On the southern wall there is an attractive memorial to Rev. Thomas Jones, 1770, a chaplain of St. Saviour's.

Above: *Almshouses of Alice Overman, on north side of St Saviour's Church*; a water-colour drawing by T.H. Shepherd, 1855. The almshouses were founded in 1771, for '4 poor widows and 4 poor maidens'. The potted plants, the tub of water, stool, cat and unusual location create an interesting composition. Three women gossip together, the fourth hovers in her doorway. Courtesy Trustees of the British Museum.

Opposite: An old French engraving showing the *Chapel of St Mary Magdalene*, demolished in 1822, and interesting foreground activity.

Lastly, we must not forget the diversity of artefacts scattered around, both decorative and functional: the great brass candelabrum on a long elaborate chain, incorporating a crown and mitre, the gift of Dorothy Appleby in 1680, hanging over the altar, the elaborately carved Elizabethan chest and the model of the sixteenth century church, with adjacent Winchester House, presented by its designer T. Keane (former Headmaster of St Saviour's School) in 1928; the Jacobean communion table, and in the Harvard Chapel the spired tabernacle by A.W. Pugin, 1851, with engraved, gem studded brass door. Also in the Harvard Chapel we will admire the embroidered wall hanging showing a variety of biblical characters on the theme 'Laborare est orare' (to work is to pray), commemorating the Church of England Working Mens Society.

Wandering around the cathedral, peering at all the things described above, we may find ourselves entering another 'time dimension', forgetting completely our own everyday preoccupations, until we remember that it is time to eat once again. As we stray away one questioning thought rises up in our consciousness: how is it possible after all this commemorated time that life still goes on, that generation still follows on after generation? Outside in the precincts, and at London Bridge, incoming and outgoing trains squeak and squeal, solitary office workers scurry home; restaurants and pubs are open for evening business. Care-free, harassed, lonely, baffled, or light-hearted people all may be glimpsed around here within a few minutes. This is a city beyond all comprehension.

Above: *The phone call*; a water-colour by George Large, 1995. The telephone box has been transposed from Tottenham Court Road, and the painting is hardly an image for the local historian concerned with topographical accuracy; however Southwark Cathedral is in the background. The disturbance of the three boys in J. Paramor's Peckham painting now becomes the acute frustration of the three youths.

Above: An etching, 1986, by Jo Winkelman: a more traditional view of the cathedral. Green Dragon Court lies to the left.

CATHEDRAL PRECINCTS I: Montague Close, St Mary Overie Dock, Clink Street

With their gardens, old schools and residences of the clergy, most English cathedral precincts strive to sustain a mood of restfulness and tranquillity: a sense that things will remain like this for ever more. At Southwark Cathedral, by way of contrast, the restless, ever changing great world is clamouring at its portals: commerce and money, property development, officialdom and power, global exploration, punishment and incarceration. Southwark Cathedral is deeply rooted in a landscape where we may ponder on many of England's past and present preoccupations and obsessions.

The landscape changed dramatically in the early 1980's with the clearance of old warehouses, opening up the view of the cathedral from across the river. Michael Twigg, Brown and Partners are the architects responsible for Minerva House, Palace House, No 2, Cathedral Street, as well as the renovation and rebuilding of Pickford's Wharf. They are also the architects of Cotton's Centre (housing Citibank and the Canadian Imperial Bank of Commerce), and Hay's Galleria on the eastern side of London Bridge. These new buildings are interesting and stimulating to look at, perhaps the best of all 1980's developments in docklands.

Minerva House has been occupied since 1983 by the Australia and New Zealand Banking Group; Palace House opposite since 1993 by DNV Industries Ltd (Det Norske Veritas), which provides services to marine, shipping and offshore industries; No 2, Cathedral Street by Addison, corporate design company since 1986. At Minerva House we will notice one solitary tree sunk in a recessed courtyard, almost encased in brickwork. If this building expresses a conformist, corporate mentality, we must remember that after all a bank is a place of employees where procedures and regulations are obligatory.

The design of the new cathedral chapter house (which incorporates a public restaurant), of 1988, architect: Ronald Sims, and built by Yorkshire masons under Tom Adamson, expresses by way of contrast a much greater individuality: a low rise, dumpy complex of two connected blocks conveys a sense of human diversity and community, a theme admirably developed by Jen Parker in her commemorative drawing showing the personalities involved which hangs at the entrance to the restaurant.

Returning to Minerva House, we may pause at St Mary Overie's Dock and enjoy its reflection in the water – its U-shaped windows now upturned into arches. The dock or inlet takes its name from the old priory: 'overie' may mean quite simply 'over the water'.

Across the dock at Palace House and No 2, Cathedral Street, the tensions are more physical: we can study with interest the conflicts between brickwork, glass and open space. This setting seems altogether appropriate for the locating of the replica of Sir Francis Drake's Golden Hinde (global circumnavigation in 1577), which was floated into the dock in September 1996. It replaces the Kathleen and May now gone into a West Country maritime museum. The ship's rigging and masts bring vitality and zest into a landscape which otherwise might seem just a bit too earnest.

Ground floor arches and passageways of Palace House lead us into Clink Street. Here we may well stop suddenly in our tracks when we confront for the first time the fourteenth century remains of the great hall of Winchester Palace, London residence of the bishops of Winchester from the twelfth to the seventeenth century: a structure which seems ideal for the camera lens of tourists and art photographers alike. Pickford's Wharf warehouse, built in 1864 stored flour, hops and seed. Today, in its rebuilt form it contains private flats, shops, the offices of BZW Private Equity Ltd, Warner Carnston, The Sound Organisation London (specialist hi-fi retailers), and the old Thameside Inn. The smaller Winchester Wharf houses a variety of small businesses; on the ground floor is Backspace, opened in 1996, a 'cyber gallery', centre for access to the Internet, film makers, and poetry readings. Thrusting its publicity at us is Floatworks, a flotation tank and therapy centre. The new Clink Wharf apartments are next door to Winchester Wharf: two seven and six storey blocks with interconnecting walkways and two tall brick columns at street level.

Across the road is the Clink Prison Museum, not the original prison building, but adjacent to the site of the Bishop of Winchester's place of incarceration. A blue plaque on a surviving stretch of wall records its existence. It was finally burnt down in the 'Gordon' riots of 1780 and not rebuilt. You can read about the prison in a booklet written by E.J. Burford and published by the museum. Stoney Street comes out into Clink Street at this point and you glimpse a murky stretch of currently derelict railway arch premises on the right. We now seem far away from the open spaces, water and light of cathedral precincts, as we pass down a gloomy railway tunnel: we emerge thankfully from this dark, dank zone and find ourselves in another locality; we are now in Bank End; the Anchor Pub lies in front and a long riverside walkway opens up.

Above: A drawing by Grace Golden, c. 1920, showing *Cathedral Street and St Mary Overie Dock*. Courtesy: Southwark Local Studies Library. The South London Gallery holds other drawings of this location by Geoffrey Fletcher, Terry Frost, Dorothy Mills, and M. von Werther.

Above: *North west view of the hall of Winchester Palace, Southwark, as it appeared after the fire which happened on August 28, 1814*; engraved by B. Howlett, published by Robert Wilkinson, 1815. Courtesy: Southwark Local Studies Library.

Below: *A quaint corner of Southwark: the Anchor, Bankside*; drawing by Hanslip Fletcher.

Above: *The pilgrim comes to pray and finds himself amongst the vegetables.* A drawing by Hanslip Fletcher from his article *London's hidden cathedral*: some sketches torn from an artist's notebook, made during a walk along Bankside, published in the Pall Mall Magazine, March 8, 1912.

Above: A painting, 1980's, by Mike Challenger, showing the Stoney Street side of *Borough Market*, the nineteenth century Wheatsheaf pub, and Park Street beyond.

CATHEDRAL PRECINCTS II: Borough Market, Stoney Street, Cathedral Street, Park Street

'The pilgrim comes to pray and finds himself amongst the vegetables', writes Hanslip Fletcher in his 1912 Pall Mall Magazine article, and indeed this is so, so close together are the cathedral and Borough Market.

BOROUGH MARKET is sandwiched between Stoney Street and Cathedral Street (Bedale Street at its southern most end), and bisected by a railway line running from London Bridge to Cannon Street, opened in 1866. This famous fruit and vegetable market has been situated on this site since the mid eighteenth century, but dates back to the thirteenth when it stretched from London Bridge down into Borough High Street. In the Victorian period the railway works necessitated major rebuilding, 1863-64, with architectural work by Edward Habershon, followed by Henry Jarvis, Junior and Senior. The large glass dome was a feature at this time, and a local landmark which you notice in contemporary drawings. A twentieth century development has been the replacement of Three Crown Court (admirably illustrated in a drawing by Hubert Williams and also drawn by Hanslip Fletcher in 1928 for the Sunday Times) with the new 1931 entrance, architects: A.W. Cocksey and Partners, with trust offices above.

The entangled forest of pillars and ironwork, glass and wood give much character to this close-knit trading enclave; we sense the intensity of ceaseless commerce, and the survival of traditions and practises even when we are there outside trading hours. Ever minded to ensure the survival of this ancient market, the trustees have drawn up innovative plans for new developments (exhibited at the Royal Institute of British Architects in the autumn of 1996): a new retail area is being proposed, as well as restaurants, and an entrepreneur Duncan Vaughan-Arbuckle plans a dynamic new wine museum for the Stoney Street railway arches (Southwark News, August 17, 1996). There are, indeed, impressive pub buildings around here: Southwark Tavern on the corner of Southwark Street, and further up Stoney Street the Wheatsheaf and the Market Porter. In Bedale Street there is the Globe, 1872, designed by Henry Jarvis.

PARK STREET leads off Stoney Street and has domestic and commercial buildings of varying periods. On the corner is a Queen Anne block from 1887-88, architects: Edward L'Anson and Edward Haslehurst. Numbers 1-13 form a long terrace, dated 1831, by Henry Rose; at number 11 is the Borough Café, established in 1831, and at number one the Market Brewery, established in 1981. There is another nineteenth century terrace at numbers 22-26. The upper part of Park Street is dominated by new housing to the left, and a business complex to the right at number 29 with orange and black tiling. This area has, however, important historical associations: Thomas Cure's College almshouses, dating back to 1584, stood at the lower end of Park Street and he is recorded on a plaque above number seven. Park Street continued formerly as Deadman's Place: a centre for religious non-conformity. The Independent Meeting House was here until 1788, with its own burial ground, becoming later the Pilgrim Fathers' Memorial Church; also here were the old Park Meeting House of the Quakers, and the Baptist Chapel and school in Zoar Street. This is also the site of the Anchor Brewery, and a new plaque records its succession of brewers and owners, starting with the Monger family 1616-70, becoming Barclay Perkins & Co from 1781 to 1955, and then amalgamating with Courage's in Bermondsey. Both breweries were finally closed in 1982. At the top end of Porter Street there is a plaque to Dr Johnson – he often visited Mrs Thrale and her husband Henry Thrale, one of the eighteenth century owners, at their home in Park Street. At the Southwark Bridge end of Park Street (this part formerly known as Maid Lane) you will find the plaque commemorating the Globe Theatre, placed here in 1908 (temporarily removed).

42

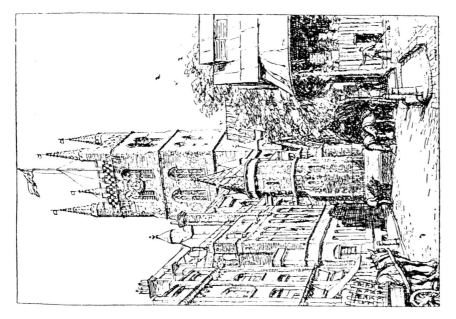

Above: *Site of old market offices*; a drawing by Hubert Williams, 1920's. Courtesy: Southwark Local Studies Library. The view is of Winchester Walk towards Cathedral Street.

Opposite: *View in Three Crown Court, High Street, with a statue of King Charles II removed from the old Town Hall in 1793*; water-colour by T.H. Shepherd. 1840. Courtesy: Trustees of the British Museum.

Above: *Thomas Cure's almshouses, Park Street*; water-colour drawing by T.H. Shepherd, 1852. Courtesy: Trustees of the British Museum. Established in 1584, rebuilt in 1831, moved to West Norwood with the coming of the Charing Cross Railway.

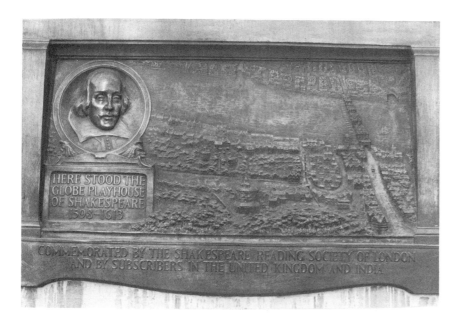

Above: *The plaque commemorating the Globe Theatre*, near its original site in Park Street, erected in 1908; designed by E. Lanteris, executed by William Martin (currently removed for building work). The Shakespeare Reading Society of London was formed in 1875 and is still active.

Opposite: *St Peter Church, Sumner Street*;
the Penny Magazine, December 31, 1839.
Below: *Entrance to Barclay's Brewery*; from
Penny Magazine, March 27, 1841. A descrip
article, with four interior views appeared in
Illustrated London News, February 6, 1847.
illustrated booklet history was published by
firm in 1951.

Below: An interior view of the school connected
with and under part of the *Baptist chapel (John
Bunyan's Meeting House), in Zoar Street,
Gravel Lane*; drawn by Schnebbelie, engraved
by Dale and published by R. Wilkinson, 1822.
The print also shows the meeting house in use as
a millwright's shop. An exterior view of the
chapel, with map, was published by Wilkinson
in 1814.

SOUTHWARK STREET: The hard world

This is a street of imposing Victorian warehouses, blocks of modern offices, and people in employment. The government block St Christopher's House, 1959, architect: Morris de Metz, is a dominating presence here; but perhaps it is the people you notice here first on a week day: they are not for the most part self-employed people, struggling to make ends meet, devising feasible enterprises, searching endlessly for new custom, but people who are able to fit themselves into conglomerate hierarchy; obedient, willing, but perhaps ultimately indifferent. No employee wants to stand about looking at his or her environment, but Southwark Street overwhelms anyone interested in Victorian architecture with the magnificent old hop exchange building, 1866, architect: R.H. Moore, at its eastern end; we can best admire the exterior from across the street, but access to the central hall, with balconies and offices leading off three floors is permitted only to those on business here. Progressing down the street we can admire number 49, of 1867, with its rounded street corners and contrasting sets of windows; next to it numbers 51-53, five-storeyed, and currently empty; number 59 breaks up the monotony of endless repetitive detail with its ornate doorway (now a window), and its set of pilasters on three storeys. Numbers 89, 97 and 99 come into view next and likewise impress with their grandeur. Number 97, 1867-68, architect Edward Cresy, the younger, is a very early example of a now disused Metropolitan Fire Brigade fire station. In 1899-90 it was converted by LCC into Holmwood Buildings. No 99, 1873, architect: T.R. Smith, houses offices of the Waterman Partnership, consulting engineers, and the Kirkaldy's Testing Museum. David Kirkaldy, his son and grandson were involved with their materials testing business here from 1874 until 1965 and on the pediment over the main door is his motto 'Facts not opinions'. The double doors at ground level give access to the main testing room which still houses Kirkaldy's unique materials testing machine.

Perambulating Southwark Street one may have a sense of dread and nothingness, a sense that there in this street laid out in 1864, the first street to be made by the Metropolitan Board of Works, our presence is of no account; or else, depending on our mood we may be struck by the grandeur and futility of commercial London past and present, its relentless piling up and dispersal of goods and the accumulation of wealth, its frenetic, driving energy, its endless construction, demolition and rebuilding and changing of hands, and its wave upon wave of workers,

As is so often in London, however, a dramatic contrast of atmosphere is at hand. If we retrace our steps eastwards and stray into Hopton Street we can sink into the stillness and peace emanating from Hopton's almshouses. Erected in 1752 in accordance with the will of Charles Hopton, a fishmonger, we are consoled by the sense that the twentieth century may have been just one gigantic aberration. Across the road is the monstrous, submarine-like Sampson House, part of Lloyds Bank, and nearby the Bankside Lofts site, incorporating renovated Victorian and twentieth century commercial blocks, and the newly built Millennium Tower. Amidst all this is number 61 Hopton Street, of about 1700.

Above: *Lamp and ventilating shaft erected over the subway, Southwark Street*; executed by Messrs. Walter Macfarlane & Co, under the direction of Mr Bazalgette; from the Builder, January 14, 1865. A somewhat surreal image, with transfixed persons and dog. Another version of the subject, with bustling street scene was published in the Illustrated London News, February 18, 1865.

Above: *The new Hop and Malt Exchange, Southwark Street*; from the Penny Illustrated Paper, October 26, 1867; architect: R.H. Moore.
Stanley Anderson's etching on the back cover shows the present-day building: without the turret and the topmost floor.

Above: *Interior of the Hop and Malt Exchange building;* from the Builder, October 5, 1867.

Above: An engraving from the 1875 Spring catalogue of *Waite, Burnell and Huggins*, seed growers and merchants, at 79 Southwark Street.

Above: *Southwark Street*, 1970; a drawing by Norman Janes. Courtesy: South London Gallery. The tower of St Thomas' Church is in the background.

Above: *Offices of a well-known Victorian publisher*; an engraving from their 1907-08 catalogue.

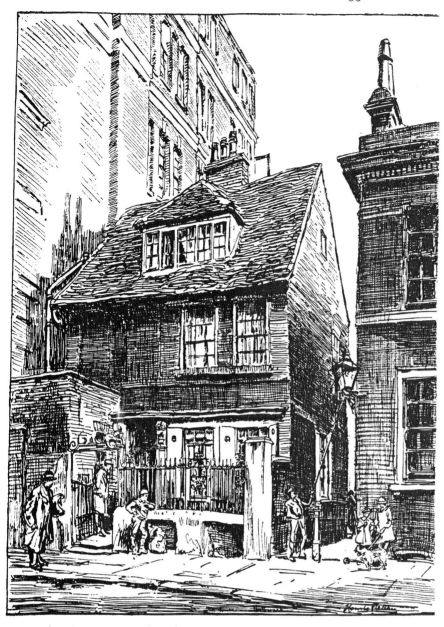

Above: *A Southwark survival: the little house in Holland Street, formerly Green Walk*; a drawing by Hanslip Fletcher. The street is now Hopton Street; the house at number 61 has had a variety of tenants since the eighteenth century (see Survey of London: Bankside).

Opposite: The decorated pediment over the main entrance to the hall of the old *Hop Exchange* (shown in the engraving from the Builder).

Above: *Warehouse, Southwark New Street*; architect: Mr. Wimble, from the Builder, January 27, 1868. The entrance gate leads the eye upwards to the eccentric gable and turret. The building seems to be full of staring, troubled eyes.

RIVERSIDE PROMENADE 1: Visitors, pubs, churches and bridges

A Sunday afternoon is a good time for your Bankside Promenade; then the place will be free of its stressed-out, high-flying executives, and its demon runners, then the place is given over to boy and girl friends on their bicycles and roller skates, to middle class people from the provinces and from overseas, here in pursuit of culture and the area's theatrical associations. Bankside is a very ancient river wall walkway, known earlier simply as 'The Banck'. Once Bankside had many taverns; today there are only two: the Anchor which welcomes us to Bankside as we emerge from Clink Street, and the Founders Arms opposite Bankside Gallery. Cardinal's Cap Alley is on the site of the Cardinal's Hat, and the Falcon is commemorated by the block of flats Falcon Point at the Blackfriars Bridge end. The nineteenth century Welsh Trooper stood at number 37, on the corner of what was then Emerson Street, and was recorded by J.T. Wilson in the 1860's in an attractive watercolour held by Southwark Local Studies Library.

Although we have had the Tate for many years, Shakespeare for even longer, the powers that be are excited by the emerging new Bankside cultural complex dominated by the new Tate Gallery in the old power station, and the brand new Globe Theatre, buildings and facilities which fill in the range of cultural provision between the South Bank Centre and the Design Museum and the art galleries at Butlers Wharf to the east, and which help to open up a long riverside stretch from Westminster to Bermondsey. All these middle class visitors come no doubt for culture which will confirm their middle class status: culture which helps them to get on in life. If they are up from the provinces or come from overseas, they are not here to ponder on what it means to live in London, to be enmeshed in its manic energy, its desperate rat race mentality, its terrifying unconcern for human predicaments, do not wish to ponder on those who have to embark on the nightmarish search for a place to live in, a place to work at, or some kind of employment, the finding of friends, and a sense of belonging. They do not wish to know of the dread felt by every insecure Londoner of being thrown out onto the streets and left to die of cold and starvation. The academic mind does not concern itself with such considerations.

At Bankside we can perhaps escape temporarily from such neuroses, remind ourselves that the City of London lying there across the river was once a place full of elegant church spires. Before the Great Fire of London of 1666 there were 97 churches within the city's walls; today, there are only 38; today, they have been brutally pushed aside by modern day developments, yet from Bankside many spires are visible, they beckon to us to come over and have a look, remind us that even if we are Londoners, the city still has a rich treasury of fine church buildings. If our promenade has taken us to Blackfriars Bridge, looking eastwards, we can identify: St Benet's, St Michael Cole Abbey (never an abbey in fact, the origin of the name is obscure), St Mary Somerset (tower only, name probably derived from a nearby wharf Somershithe), St Mary le Bow, St Mary Aldermary, St James Garlickhythe, the twin towers of Cannon Street Station (they are part of the original station, not of a church), St Magnus the Martyr (close to the Monument), St Dunstans in the East (tower only, with beautiful garden attached), All Hallows (at Tower Hill).

Looking downstream, we are reminded that this stretch of water has a set of five bridges: Blackfriars Road Bridge, Blackfriars Railway Bridge, Southwark Bridge, Cannon Street Railway Bridge, and London Bridge. We are engaged, perhaps, with only two of them: interesting, blown up artwork is to be found under Blackfriars Bridge tunnel (the second bridge was built 1860-69, designed by Joseph Cubitt and H. Carr, replacing the Robert Mylne bridge of 1760-9); here we may enjoy lingering over the reproductions of old engravings from the Illustrated London News. Southwark Bridge of today was built 1912-21, architect: Sir Ernest George, replacing the Rennie Bridge built 1814-19, of Little Dorrit fame. As we trot back home, or towards London Bridge, we may stop in our tracks if we are observant as we pass through the underpass to admire the carved relief work on the wall: an eighteenth century map, and carvings by Richard Kindersley of scenes of Thames frost fairs. This is an initiative of Groundwork Southwark.

RIVERSIDE PROMENADE II: Art gallery

On another Sunday afternoon, our promenade may take us down to the Bankside Gallery, home of the Royal Watercolour Society, founded in 1804, and the Royal Society of Painter-Engravers, founded in 1880. Here in this intimate gallery, we will often find exhibitions overflowing with talent, and prodigious technical virtuosity. Talks and guided tours are often arranged in the evenings, and on many occasions you may meet people you would never meet elsewhere: connoisseurs and collectors, knowledgeable people from other walks of life, and artists themselves. There was the stunning show of Russian and Ukraine prints organised by Peter Ford from Bristol, when Russian printmakers spoke to the assembled gathering through an interpreter. Several years later I came here to listen to Hilary Paynter, wood engraver of genius, speak of her own work and that of colleagues; I sat here one evening listening to Chris Orr talking of his own work, as the slides clicked in and out with manic insistence, he told us how 30 years on he sensed he was only just beginning, yet was aware too that life does not go on for ever.

This is the driven world of those born to be artists, gifted individuals in the grip of a talent which will not relinquish its demands, a talent which they are powerless to withstand. Yet, in all places where artistic talent abounds, there is unease: between artists themselves, between artists and administrators, between artists and all those joined by invisible threads: clients, collectors, publishers, writers, curators and all those who are simply curious and wish to be connected to this enchanted world; the world of the visual artist inspires a complex web of emotions: of delight and fascination, of desperation and inferiority.

We may depart home from such occasions curiously elated, yet also full of introspective doubts as to what we ourselves have actually achieved in our own lives.

Above: *The Founders Arms, Holland Street*; architect: William C. Banks; from the Builder, February 19, 1881. The present-day building is much less grandiose and stands at the riverside, facing the Bankside Gallery.

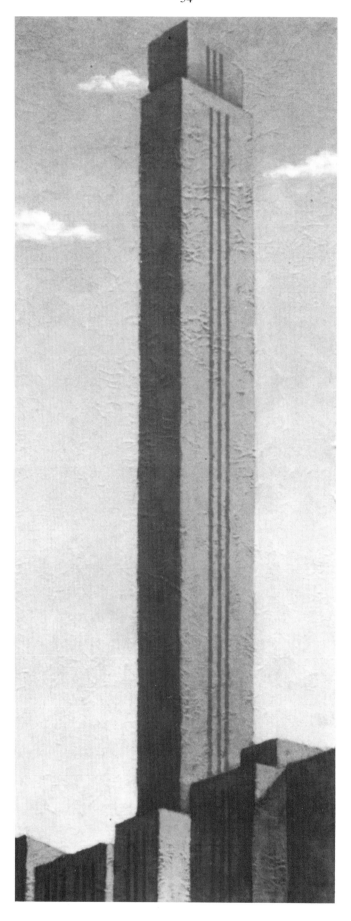

Above: *Bankside*, oil painting, 1995, of the chimney of Bankside Power Station, by Rod Judkins. Built in 1963, architect: Sir Giles Gilbert Scott, on the site of Bankside Gasworks, then Phoenix Gas Works, then the City of London Electric Lighting Co Ltd. The site was originally Great Pike Gardens. Work is currently in progress on the conversion of this edifice into the new Tate Gallery of Modern Art (designed by Jacques Herzog and Pierre de Meuron).

South London Gallery has a drawing by Geoffrey Fletcher, 1957, of the chimney under construction.

Artists have been active drawing the old pre-conversion interior, and the etching on the following page is by Olwen Jones.

56

Above: *The great fire at Bankside on Friday night, Saturday 16th February, 1855*; from the Illustrated London News, February 24, 1855. An engraving of almost surreal quality depicting a fire which started at the timber yard and steam saw mill of Messrs.

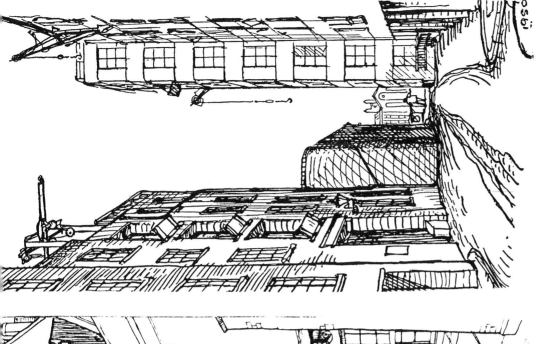

Above: *Bear Gardens, Sunday afternoon, 1950;* drawing by Grace Golden from her *Old Bankside*.

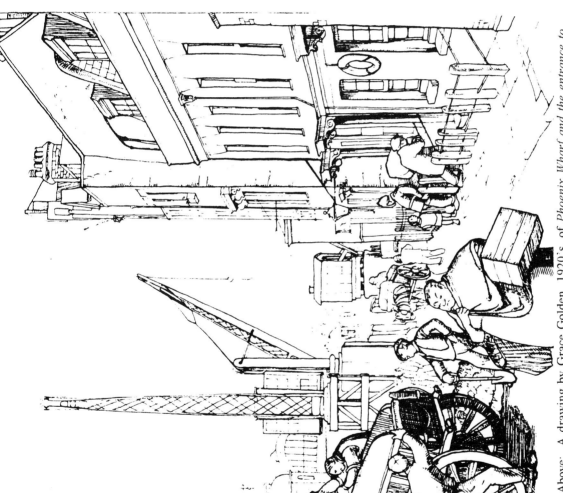

Above: A drawing by Grace Golden, 1920's, of *Phoenix Wharf and the entrance to Cardinal Cap Alley.* Courtesy: Southwark Local Studies Library. The alley dates back to the end of the sixteenth century. No 49 is late 17th, early 18th century and was owned by Sells, coal merchants until 1873, and is now a private residence. No's 50-52 were built in 1712 and until the early 20th century occupied by coal and iron merchants, coppersmiths, lightermen, glass and lamp manufacturers; since 1958 lodgings of the Provost of Southwark Cathedral. The present-day buildings have been remodelled since this drawing.

Above: *Rose Alley, from Park Street, 1926;* drawing by Grace Golden, from her *Old Bankside*.

PENETRATING BANKSIDE: Some facts and observations

If, after our riverside promenade we should decide to penetrate the Bankside locality, we will experience a stabbing sense of topographical confusion. We are quite right to ask whether the City of London has invaded this patch, tidied it up, brought in whole armies of regimented people who are quite different from those who worked in the old Bankside trades and industries. The part of Park Street which runs behind Bankside is dominated today by two sprawling bank developments: Lloyds at Red Lion Court, and Midland at numbers 62-72, the latter built in 1991 as the bank's central cheque clearing facility. Opposite at number 185 is National Grid, and eastwards on the corner of Emerson Street is the Insurance Ombudsman Bureau at number 135.

Emerson Street was formerly Thames Street. Today its uppermost end has been renamed New Globe Walk, leading as it does to the reconstructed Globe Theatre complex. The Inigo Jones indoor theatre is in New Globe Walk. Benbow House at the riverside, built in 1968, is named after the James Benbow Iron Foundry here from the 1840's to the 1880's, previously Bradley and Benbow Eagle Foundry, and in the 1790's Mr Bradley's foundry. This foundry was on both sides of Bear Gardens, the next alley eastwards.

Bear Gardens is important as the site of the Hope Theatre, which flourished for several years, 1614-16, at the time when the Globe was being rebuilt after its fire. It staged the first performance of Ben Johnson's Bartholomew Fair in 1614. Philip Henslowe and Jacob Meade acquired the bear baiting ring which was here from about 1546 and continued this entertainment in their new theatre. Bear Gardens closed about 1670, but others continued until as late as 1835 when the sport was at last forbidden by law; but could one suggest that a lust for blood still flows on – lurking with persistence in the background of all our present day sports and entertainments? Another theatre, the Davies' Amphitheatre, was here later, between 1662 and 1682, built by James Davies. The White Bear Pub was here from 1832-1929, and the old Bankside firm Porn & Dunwoody Ltd (lift manufacturers) have their premises on the site. Opposite is an old tea warehouse, a listed building and empty for some years now. Number one Bear Gardens was the site of William Field, coffee roasters from 1906-51, and since 1972 has been occupied by the Bear Gardens Museum, and since 1994 the Globe Education Centre. The new Bankside complex will eventually house all its facilities and functions together.

Rose Alley is important as the site of the first Bankside theatre which flourished here from 1587 to 1603. It was built by Philip Henslowe and his partner John Cholmley.

Wandering around these dismal alleys and gloomy streets, one thought seems to emerge: is it possible that the theatrical profession requires such an atmosphere of darkness and emptiness in which to flourish? Is it possible that out of this nothingness everything emerges with the utmost theatricality?

opposite and below: *The Globe Theatre*: three prints by distinguished members of the Royal Society of Painter-printmakers.
opposite: *Thatching the Globe*, wood engraving by Sarah van Niekerk, 1995. London's first thatched building since the 1666 Great Fire.
below, left: *Early stage*, etching, 1994, by Jo Winkelman. A much larger print by the same artist (53cm x 34cm) shows the wooden seating structure at a more advanced stage of construction, with St Paul's Cathedral in the background.
below, right: *The Globe*, wood engraving by Hilary Paynter.

Sam Wanamaker established his Globe Playhouse Trust in 1970 to raise funds for the rebuilding, which finally got underway in 1992. In October 1995 £12.4 million of National Lottery funding was granted to the Trust to fund the completion of the Globe, the Inigo Jones indoor theatre, foyer areas and ancillary facilities. In the summer of 1996 the prologue season staged The Two Gentlemen of Verona, and the opening festival is planned for June 1997. The Globe is one of six buildings on a 1.2 acre site that together will form the International Shakespeare Globe Centre. Friends of Shakespeare's Globe support the project, and there are over 5,000 members world-wide.

Below: *Messrs. James Epps & Co's Steam Cocoa Mills, Holland Street*; architect: Edwin T. Hall: from Building News, December 20, 1878. Erected on the site previously occupied by the Falcon Glass Works. James Epps introduced cocoa as a popular drink in Britain; he died in 1907 and is buried at Norwood Cemetery.

RIVERSIDE PROMENADE III: In Oxo Towerland (Coin Street redevelopment site)

Housing co-ops in trendy new architecture, Bernie Spain Gardens, craft and designer shops, the newly refurbished Oxo Tower Wharf, summertime festivals, a riverside walk: all new and recent developments between Waterloo and Blackfriars Bridges. Something unusual is going on: all these developments come not from the powers that be as one might expect in a region dominated by all those initials: IBM, IPC, LWT, but from a non-profit organisation, Coin Street Community Builders, formed in 1984 for the purchase and redevelopment of 13 acres of land, and consisting of people all actually living in Waterloo and Blackfriars.

I requested publicity information from the public relations officer at their current headquarters at 99 Upper Ground, and through the post came their elephantine, over-the-top brochure on Oxo Tower Wharf, with dramatic aerial views; my desk was hardly big enough for their July 1996 South Bank News printed on large pastel coloured folio sheets. Here I felt was an organisation which was immensely proud and sure of its activities.

The housing project is extensive and will eventually involve seven different sites: all will be run as co-ops and will be named after trees. The Mulberry Co-op was built in 1988, a project of the Coin Street Design Team and built around a central childrens' play area. The Broadwall site, the Palm Co-op, was completed in 1994, architects: Lifschutz Davidson. Its innovative and interesting use of different materials: wood, brick and metal, and the juxtaposition of the nine-storey tower block with the adjacent terrace have produced a complex which has been recognised with design prizes from the Royal Fine Art Commission, the Sunday Times, RIBA, and the Civic Trust. You can read an evaluation in Architecture Today, issue 52, October 1994. Redwood Co-op occupies five floors of Oxo Tower Wharf; the Lime Co-op will be built on a site at the corner of Bargehouse Crescent and Upper Ground. Looking further ahead there will be other developments on the car park site west of Mulberry, with community facilities, at Gabriel's Wharf and behind the National Theatre in Upper Ground.

In the midst of it all are the Bernie Spain Gardens, commemorating one of the original campaigners; approached from Stamford Street and extending across Upper Ground to the riverside walk, these community gardens are a delight for every jaded city dweller.

Oxo Tower Wharf started as a power generating station for the Post Office; it was built in 1928 as a cold store and processing plant for the Oxo Company; the tower spells out the name OXO with its geometric windows and was added in 1930. Today, after many years of semi-dereliction, the complex is set to become a new centre for contemporary design; visitors can meet, buy and commission from talented designers in the 33 retail workshops here, including winners of the new Sainsbury scholarships. On the roof top around the tower a new Harvey Nichols restaurant has just opened, and there is also a public viewing gallery; a riverside café-bar is due to open soon on the second floor, and a ground floor mall will be used for music and theatre performances. In addition, five floors are devoted to co-op housing, and there will also be a number of retail shops.

Next to Oxo Tower Wharf is Sea Containers House, with golden balls at its corners, built in the early 1980's, and headquarters for Sea Containers Group (marine, leisure and travel interests), and premises of HM Customs & Exise, legal, surveying and publishing firms. At the eastern end of Stamford Street, on the corner of Rennie Street, there is Stamford House, built 1912-13, and registered offices of J. Sainsbury PLC.

During the summer months the area explodes into sound and colour and the Coin Street Festival is staged; it is now in its seventh year. In 1996 there were events such as 'Spring Greens' (three days of 'inspiration, solutions, and alternatives for a greener world'), a celebration of football art and culture, a Brazilian carnival, and a weekend Latin American fiesta. I came here on August 15th for the Greek music and dance. I stood in the crowd with all kinds of other people and listened to the hypnotic rhythms, the surging melodies expressing energy and sadness, watched the musicians playing bagpipes, violin and drum. The swaying, tender dances of solicitude of the women in yellow and black costumes contrasted with the self-centred belligerence of the male dancers, yet they would all come together, clasp hands in dances of faith and celebration. In the shops all around I felt I was encountering a somewhat more fragile world: temporary shops run by designer crafts people selling ceramics, wooden toys, hand-painted silks, jewellery, and scattered around, wood sculpture by Friedel Buecking.

Returning home that August afternoon I seemed to stray from one world to another: away from arts and crafts, and back into London's hard world of media nuts, strutting lawyers, calculating officials. As I scurried away, I thought about a large print called 'Lino Man' by Ron Henocq which I had seen earlier at the Café Gallery in Southwark Park. Are we all like this today in England, I wondered? Steam-rollered, dice throwing, scratching out numbers on lottery cards, flattened out figures, hearts cancelled out, devoid of direction and purpose, given over to games of chance?

Returning home to Bermondsey I felt almost invisible; someone not seen and of no account to the businessmen, the tourists, the planners and folk dancers. I noticed that a new café-cum-pub the Honest Cabbage had opened in the premises of the former Yorkshire Grey; Dolomore, drinks importer had just closed its operations: all its windows were covered with corrugated iron; its forecourt had emptied quite suddenly.

I returned to a glass of ice cold Amberdown cider and Symphonie Fantastique by Berlioz.

Above: *Hopton Street, Bankside*; wood engraving by Sarah van Niekerk. The Bankside Gallery lies to the north. The grotesque branches mock the angular buildings; the pigeons outnumber the solitary figure; a bleak, desolate winter scene. The Bankside Power Station is in the background, in the foreground nineteenth century premises currently occupied by David Mussett Ltd, paper merchants (previously a tannery and a wheelwright's).

IN THE LAND OF GRIEF: In and around Southwark Bridge Road

If we are seeking an intimate place to go for silence and reflection, we might stray into the tiny garden of All Hallows Church in Copperfield Road. The church was originally built in 1879-80, architect: G.G. Scott, Junior, a vast, impressive building, but destroyed in World War II. A new church was built in 1957, architect: T.F. Ford and this building now houses a recording studio. The fragmented remains of the old church – several arches, part of a chapel with crucifix, the boarded up Edwardian Post Office building (awaiting conversion into an arts centre) at the top of Pepper Street, the empty Fox and Hounds pub, 1884, all create a mood of gentle sadness, a sense that a certain period of time has closed. Local workers and residents come to the garden at mid-day: to eat lunch, to do a crossword, puff at a cigarette, wait for a friend; and people full of grief come here to let their emotions dissolve in the sun, into the yellow daisies, fuschias, and hollyhocks in this tiny garden.

The Borough Welsh Congregational Chapel, 1872-73, architect: Thomas Thomas and the adjacent house are decked out with flowers; steps and doorways covered with petunias, convovuli, and flowering shrubs in such profusion as if these were the floral tributes to a departed person. At number 88, the Corner Shop is selling miscellaneous bric-a-brac: junk to us perhaps, but things which may have helped to make life more bearable, less frightening, more manageable to someone.

An adventure playground, little corner shops, old fire brigade buildings, a library of 1898, architect: E.J. Phipps, now the Borough Community Centre with a 1950's ambience café in the basement; a park where the Mint Street slum once was, haunted by the underworld: the moods of this place are confused and contradictory.

You will also find charitable organisations around here: in Copperfield Street beyond Winchester Cottages (built 1893-95), the United Kingdom Band of Hope Union; in Loman Street the National Alcohol and Drug Resource Centre; in Great Guildford Street at Fenner Brockway House, War on Want; and the National Foster Care Association at 5-7 Marshalsea Road. Progressing up Southwark Bridge Road, the League Against Cruel Sports is at number 91. Taking up worthy causes is perhaps one way to escape from one's own problems into something much bigger; another way is to search out art which enables us to transcend the smallness and aloneness of ourselves. Printmakers have studies at Globe Studios, at number 62 Southwark Bridge Road, and I went there one traumatic day to visit Brenda Hartill who showed me her series of gigantic prints, composite train and townscape creations, reworking motives from the local environment and Waterloo Railway Station.

The Southwark Playhouse is also at this address. It is currently being refurbished with a generous arts lottery grant. Its productions are from world theatre, and remind us of the existence of diverse unexplored dramatical talents.

Progressing further up Southwark Bridge Road we will encounter Anchor Terrace on our right, dating from 1834, and the former headquarters of Courage Brewery; it currently awaits redevelopment. A TV series 'This Life' about young lawyers was filmed here. It is a large terrace with an interesting mixture of stone balustrades and iron railings. Behind the terrace lies Gatehouse Square, designed by GLC for the London Borough of Southwark in 1987. There are pavement mosaics designed and made by local Southwark schools, and in the centre of the square an interesting sculpture 'Great oaks from little acorns grow', by Brian Yale.

Across the road is Rose Court, the headquarters of the Health and Safety Executive. In the garden outside there are four lumps of rock, piles of stone and a plaque recording a tragic death in 1990 when building construction was taking place. We live in a terrifying and precarious world.

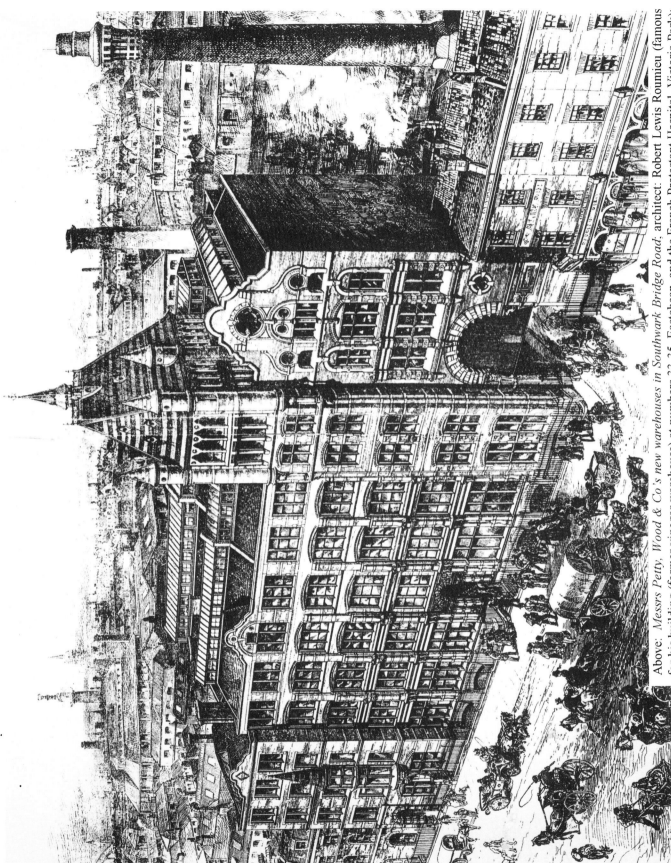

Above: *Messrs Petty, Wood & Co's new warehouses in Southwark Bridge Road*, architect: Robert Lewis Roumieu (famous for his building (former vinegar warehouse) at numbers 33-35, Eastcheap, and the French Protestant Hospital, Victoria Park); from the Builder, 1879. This rather impressive building for a confectionery manufacturer was demolished 1981-82. The

Above: *New Central Fire Brigade Station, Southwark Bridge Road*; architect: George Vulliamy; from the Builder, June 15, 1878. The initials over the doors signify: Metropolitan Fire Brigade and its controlling body the Metropolitan Board of Works. The Brigade, established in 1865, with Captain Eyre Massey Shaw as its commander moved from 68 Watling Street in the City to the above premises in 1878. The 1883 Gothic building (see Pictorial World illustration) was added as an extension to the above, and the final extension to the south was added in 1910-11, architect: W.E. Brooks.

Above: An unusual sculpture *Great oaks from little acorns*, by Brian Yale in Gatehouse Square, close to the FT building, conveying a sense of the fragility of individual enterprise.

Above: The currently empty pub *Fox & Hounds*, on the corner of Copperfield Road.

Above: *Metropolitan Fire Brigade: sketches at headquarters*; fro[m] Pictorial World, July 17, 1884.

Left: Passing a man down inside escape, from a window; Wat[er] tower.

Above: Horse on duty; fireman in drill dress; fireman in full dress.

Also illustrated in article: jumping into a sheet; and taking escape t[o] a fire, lowering it as if going under a bridge.

67

Above: *The 1883 Central Fire Brigade Station building*: architect: Robert Pearsall: from *Pictorial World*, July 17, 1884. Demolished in 1969, but a portion of the entrance way has been preserved in the front garden, together with a bell from the City HQ building. The building visible today is Winchester House, Captain Shaw's residence and a training school, built 1823-26, fronting a 1777 workhouse, later a hat factory. The watch-tower can be glimpsed from Marshalsea Road. Southwark Training Centre and the Heritage Collection Museum are based here today.

Further information on Captain Shaw can be found in Ronald Cox's biography *Oh, Captain Shaw, the life story of the first and most famous chief of the London Fire Brigade*, published by Victor Green in 1984.

BLACKFRIARS ROAD BLUES: Depression Day

Perambulating Blackfriars Road is a truly dreadful thing to do: almost a mile long, it leads down from Blackfriars Bridge to St George's Circus. Built in 1770-1800 and until 1829 known as Great Surrey Street, it has been much rebuilt in post-war years, with many offices and blocks. A city that puts up buildings which people find ugly, do not enjoy working in, and which sends people away in the evening feeling wretched must be a city which has got it all wrong.

By the bridge we find the cold, grey slabs of Express Newspapers, Ludgate House, built 1989, and opposite, nearby, the equally cold Friar Bridge Court, housing five railway companies, with the modern day Prince William Henry pub across the road. At the end of the road there is the monstrous student block McLaren House, facing BT's Hill House, and the smaller block Erlang House next to it, part of South Bank University. This is a street given over to the hard world, a place, one might think, where those who hit hardest win in the game of life.

Opposite Orbit House, the Seifert block housing the Oriental and Indian Office collections of the British Library, we find the Ring pub, full of photographs of boxers on its walls. On the corner of Nicholson Street the old Southwark College building has a plaque recording Mary Wollstonecroft (1757-97) and her 'Vindication of the rights of women' written nearby. On the corner of Webber Street there is a business centre, the Blackfriars Foundry.

Feeling numb with the impersonality and emptiness of this road, I strayed into the Peabody buildings: six blocks face the main road, the second and third blocks are joined by the entrance arch, and the initial 'P' can be observed on the gables of these two. This is a huge site, housing many hundreds of people you and I will never know. The Queen came here in 1962 to unveil a plaque commemorating the centenary of the Peabody Donation Fund (responsible for maintaining the estates today). Outside the Estate Office stood a proud black pussy cat with a luxurious white bib, standing there like an Egyptian mummy cat on guard. You must talk to such mysterious creatures, pay them your respects, and the cat winked at me, and walked away into the doorway, and I could go home a little less heavy hearted.

BLACKFRIARS ROAD: Another day, another look

Living in a city as gigantic as London, it is perhaps inevitable that we project our ever changing moods and states of mind onto things and people we encounter everyday. In a hugue city where there can be no norms, no time honoured paths through life, aimlessness and loneliness can easily engender eccentricity and a 'me' dominated outlook, each and every city dweller at the centre of a self-made universe.

On another day, refusing to accept the cold, hard face of Blackfriars Road, I was more intent on penetrating the side streets. In Nicholson Street we find buildings belonging to the Edward Edwards estate (charity founded in 1717): the reconstructed almshouses, rebuilt in 1973 and in Chancel Street the former Albert Institute, now occupied by the Electoral Reform Society. Opposite the almshouses are three terraces of differing lengths of attractive low rise housing completed in 1975, architects: Richard Sheppard, Robson and Partners. If we stray southwards into Gambia Street, we find an attractive old pub the Hop Pole.

Progressing further down Blackfriars Road we find Nelson Square. At number 44 are the headquarters of the wide ranging community organisation the Blackfriars Settlement. It has flourishing advice, education, training and work centres, runs clubs and projects for children, young and elderly people. You can read its history 1887-1987 in an illustrated booklet by Gladys Barrett (cover shows a watercolour painting of the building by Olive Freeman). It has another building, the Pickwick Centre in Rushworth Street, leading of Pocock Street, and an advice centre in Walworth Road. From the Blackfriars Road end the eye is lead down the street to the wide railway arch, with Guy's Hospital beyond, and we can also glimpse the turret of St Alphege's Clergy House. Just to the south of Nelson Square at number 176 is the Edwardian building of the Sons of Temperance Friendly Society bringing a sense of swagger and pride, whereas the blocks bring nothing but nothingness and dread. The large relief carving of the friar on horseback on the Pocock Street corner of Friars House is, however, one attempt to vitalise a large block.

I had returned to Blackfriars Road to visit an important church, so had to retrace my steps. It was lunch time on a freezing cold January day, snow starting to fall; groups of laughing and chatting people were scurrying towards the Crown pub opposite Friars House. This is a pub with an attractive street facade, decorated

Above: *Central Bank of London, branch bank, Stamford Street, Blackfriars Road*; architects: Edwin Nash & W. Hilton Nash; from the Builder, February 13, 1875. This imposing building still stands, and is currently occupied by the environmental consultancy RPS, but does not have the chimney stacks shown, and there is another bay of windows on the Blackfriars Road side.

stonework over doorways and windows, and a floating crimson and golden crown as a sign, with a coloured carved crown on the pediment.

Webber Row leads off Webber Street (previously Friar Street) on this side of the road and here one will find the five blocks of the LCC estate, behind the Peabody Buildings, built in 1905-7, with shops on the ground floor of Mawdley Buildings facing Waterloo Road. The dumpy, one storey school building, with dormer windows on the corner is a Southwark Council Centre for Language in Primary Education. In Valentine Place there is an old industrial building with two dates: established 1812, rebuilt 1887 over the doorway, and in Ufford Street we find a terrace of cottages similar in style to those in Copperfield Road. At number 74 Blackfriars Road are the former premises of builders and contractors Gordon North, with two urns and supporting carved figures.

Colombo Street leads us into the territory of Christ Church. Opposite the church is a fitness and sports centre, and beyond, the Rose and Crown pub. Alexander Colombo was a bailiff of the manor 1859-63. The small street Paris Gardens is a reference to the Manor of Paris Garden which lay beyond the Bishop of Winchester's estate, and was probably named after Robert de Paris, owner of the 14th century manor house. It became a public garden in the sixteenth century and was built over at the end of the seventeenth century.

Returning to the churchyard, two curiosities catch one's eye: the old 1900 drinking fountain bequeathed by Passmore Edwards, and the ground level concrete stone cross marking the site where a wooden cross fell blazing during World War II. It lies in front of the western wing of the church's John Marshall Hall, reminding us of the church's origins in the charity founded in 1627 by John Marshall. The charity, unusually, still runs the church and has modern day offices in Newcomen Street, off Borough High Street. It was based in the 1853 building opposite (Mollison House) until 1967. The Marshall family had their manor house in this district.

If you ring the intercom bell you will be allowed to enter the church to view what must be regarded as a high point of discovery for anyone searching for Southwark inspired art. Here you can gaze with admiration at the ten stained glass windows, plus the two biblical ones in the sanctuary, depicting Southwark trades and professions past and present, designed by Fred W. Cole, and executed by J. Wipppell & Co in 1959. On the southern side engineering, hop, printing, river and office work is depicted; on the northern side we see a charlady with a bus stop scene, baking and building work, an eighteenth century mother and child with Nelson Square flats below, and a telephone engineer with the view of St Paul's below. The compositions are very dramatic and the colours are especially vibrant. The 1984/5 windows, designed by John Lawson, and made by Goddard & Gibbs lack this excitement, but nevertheless record developments since the new church opened: the establishment of the South London Industrial Mission at the church in 1967 (a team of chaplains visit many places of work to listen, understand and support), Lloyds Bank Sampson House, Sea Containers Ltd, as well as long established organisations such as Blackfriars Settlement and John Adams & Son, manufacturers of door springs.

It is likely, however, that when we first enter this church, we will not be taken in by these windows initially, but by the blown up, city landscape photograph behind the altar with a golden cross attached to its centre. The altar covering was made in 1983 and like the 1984/5 windows comments on the interconnections between the world, work place and religious faith.

Christ Church is a flourishing centre: it has three worshipping congregations; the South East London Institute for Theological Education prepares students for the ministry, a drama therapy national organisation Sesame is based here, and trade union and other organisations use the John Marshall Hall. Here you will find, attached to the wall, a striking relief sculpture by Ian Walters, 1989, based on the Wapping print workers' dispute of the mid 1980's, with a symbolic, grasping hand at the centre of tableaux depicting riots, and old and new printing technologies. You can see other examples of the sculptor's work in Central London: a bust of Nelson Mandela outside the Royal Festival Hall, a symbolic sculpture commemorating the Spanish Civil War in Jubilee Gardens, and a statue of Fenner Brockway in Red Lion Square, Holborn.

Heading northwards from the church, there are two attractive buildings close by: the former offices of the National Society of Operative Printers and Assistants at number 26, and the four storeyed pub the Paper Moon with its decorative garlands. On the corner of Stamford Street is the old bank building, well illustrated in the Builder, and next door at number 3, another Victorian block, originally Tress House, a hat factory; used by Sainsbury's as a laboratory in post-war years, then purchased by GLC in 1980 and occupied by Elephant Jobs, a local employment scheme and recently sold to Fuller, Smith and Turner, brewers in Hammersmith who will open a pub and hotel here shortly. Such is the ever changing use of London's buildings.

Above: *Christ Church*; an etching by Preston, from a drawing by W. Pearson, 1810. A print of a drawing by C. Burton, 1827, shows the whole building and surrounding churchyard; a variety of depictions of the church, including a painting by A.C. Hart after T.H. Shepherd hang in the lounge of the church. The above is the second church, built 1738-42, replacing the 1671 church after it sank into the riverside mud. The present-day church dates from 1960, architects: R. Paxton Watson & B. Costin.

Above: *Watch House, Collingwood Street*; pencil drawing, c. 1930 by Joan Bloxam. Courtesy: London Borough of Lambeth Archives Department. The inscribed stone tablet over the doorway, dated 1819, has been preserved on the side of the rectory which now occupies the site.

73

Above: *Fishermen's Cottages, Collingwood Street;* a drawing, 1920's, by Hubert Williams. Courtesy: Southwark Local Studies Library. The street is now named Colombo Street; the cottages have gone.

Above: *The Leverian Museum (or The Rotunda), Blackfriars Road;* water-colour drawing by T.H. Shepherd, 1850; courtesy: Trustees of the British Museum. The artist has misspelt the name: the museum was named after Sir Ashton Lever who amassed his collection in the 1760's. It was sold in 1784 to a law stationer James Parkinson who moved it to the above purpose-built site. The collection was sold off in 1806. The building was then occupied by the Surrey Institution until 1820, and then used for meetings and concerts and closed in 1883; it was used for storage until demolition in 1958. There is a commemorative plaque on the wall of Drury House, off Stamford Street.

Above: *The Albert Institute*; from *Archeology and architecture of Southwark and elsewhere* sketched or designed by C.N. McIntyre North (1886). The Institute was established by a rector of Christ Church, Blackfriars Road, Rev. Joseph Brown to provide baths, meeting and club rooms, living rooms for married couples, and a dormitory for single men. It stood for some years in Gravel Lane,

Opposite: *South Metropolitan Temperance Hall*; architect: J.H. Swan, from the Illustrated London News, August 7, 1875. Erected by the London and Provincial Temperance Halls Company as 'a place of wholesome and cheerful entertainment'. Situated between Peabody Dwellings and the Surrey Theatre.

Above: *No 176, Blackfriars Road*: the London office of the society was founded in 1867 and moved here in 1904. A new building, architect: Arthur C. Russell was erected in 1910.

Above: *A new public library for Southwark*; from the London Argus, June 25, 1898. The library stood at number 179, just south of Nelson Square.

Above: Surrey Chapel, Blackfriars Road (Rowland's Chapel); from the Illustrated London News, May 7, 1881 (with factual article). The chapel was built in 1782-83, and closed in 1881, but not demolished as the Illustrated London News suggests; it continued in use as a warehouse (see engraving reproduced in Southwark Annual, 1905), and is remembered this century for its use as a boxing ring (see drawing in Charles Keeping's Cockney Ding Dong, 1975). It was destroyed in 1940. Rowland Hill, the chapel's first minister, is dealt with in Vernon J. Charlesworth's Rowland Hill: his life and pulpit savings, Hodder and Stoughton, 1882. The Surrey Chapel congregation moved to the newly-built Christ Church in Westminster Bridge Road in 1876, and the building was then occupied by the Primitive Methodists

W. SHAW, WHOLESALE IRONMONGER & MANUFACTURER, 253, BLACKFRIARS ROAD, LONDON.

Opposite and below: Early nineteenth century engravings of *commercial premises in Blackfriars Road*, from trade leaflets.

Opposite: An interior view of *Surrey Chapel*, c. 1830, drawn and engraved by J. Wilmshurst.

LINEN DRAPERS, SILK MERCERS &c.
53, 54 & 55, BLACKFRIARS ROAD, LONDON.

Above: *Peabody Square, Blackfriars Road*; architect: Henry A. Darbishire; from the Builder, January 13, 1872. This estate, still standing, was built on the site of the old Magdalen Hospital: sixteen four-storey blocks enclosing two quadrangles, with trees in both. An aerial view of the whole complex was published in the Illustrated London News, 1872. George Peabody (1795-1869) was an important international merchant/banker philanthropist. His Peabody Donation Fund was established in 1862 with the aim of providing inexpensive housing for

LOST IN A MAZE OF SIDE STREETS

Between Blackfriars Road, Southwark Bridge Road and Borough High Street there are many streets, short and long, where we may wander with interest and take in the diverse inner city landscape: a chaotic patchwork of cottage style dwellings, tenement blocks, workshops and small businesses, offices of organisations, pubs and cafés, often dramatised by the presence of nearby railway arches. Here one senses a more human life than that prevailing in the ugly main thoroughfares.

Wandering these streets one is struck yet again by the density and impenetrability of London. No one can surely grasp the significance of so many lives: no one can grasp how so many people are getting through life: whether painfully and with difficulty, or joyfully and with ease. No one can comprehend the peculiar preoccupations, concerns and tensions of the lives of so many people; the men of God may bend their ears and listen attentively, but even they hear only a bewildering cacophony of individual voices of many accents, timbres and persuasions. This is a city which is beyond all comprehension.

GREAT SUFFOLK STREET winds its way down from Southwark Street southwards to the junction with Borough High Street. The street, formerly Gravel Lane, dates from the late eighteenth century and commemorates the Duke of Suffolk, brother-in-law to Henry VIII whose London house was nearby. It can be studied with interest for its wide range of business premises, ranging from New Bridgewater House, a warehouse block at the Southwark Street end, to the recently arrived Bedford Hill Hallery at number 202 (formerly premises of the Folio Society). Around the White Hart pub on the corner of Bear Lane, we find Pickles take-away snacks, a printing shop, Clifford & Co solicitors, and a taxi garage followed by businesses under the railway arches: another garage Autotechnic, and Suffolk's Restaurant. Opposite at numbers 57-59 an old notice has been preserved, reminding us: 'Bacon smoking in progress', and we note that Metro Videos now occupy the premises of the Southwark Bacon Drying Co. The blue-glazed Mercury Communications building stands opposite the Garden Centre at numbers 77-83, and on the corner of Southwark Bridge Road we notice the Winchester pub, with its attractive sign showing Winchester Cathedral. Further down the road, to the left, is another pub, the Skinners Arms, with the motto 'To God only be all glory' beneath the coat of arms.

Going in the opposite direction, running from west to east are the interesting Union Street and Borough Road; here by way of contrast are thoroughfares given over to buildings of institutions and the powers that be.

UNION STREET dates back to 1781 (formerly Charlotte Street) and cuts across Great Suffolk Street, at the junction of which we find the Union Jack pub. The union of England with Scotland in 1707 and with Ireland in 1801 may be one origin of this very common street name. At the Borough High Street end there is the training centre of Price Waterhouse, accountants, whose stark towers to the north we find depicted in the drawings of David Fried and Stephen Mumberson. The modern 1980's facade, with its curious ground floor bays of wood panelled windows, hides the refurbished mid-nineteenth century hop warehouse behind. In Union Street we sense the constantly changing use of buildings in London: the 1908 old school building of St Saviour's Parochial and National Schools, with a rooftop playground, now houses the Southwark Diocesan Education Board (responsible for Church of England schools in the diocese). The school on this site dates back to 1704 and since 1977 has been in Redcross Way nearby.

Across the road are former church buildings: St Saviour's House is a former mission building, sold in the 1970's, and now the premises of the Association of Child Psychology and Psychiatry. The 1907 building described on its plaque as the Mint and Gospel Lighthouse Mission (Shaftesbury Society), later known as John Gerard House, is currently being converted into studios and flats. Contrast is afforded by commercial premises nearby: the timber business Travis Perkins disrupts the street facade with its open structure, and R.K. Burt & Co occupy the early nineteenth century panelled building at numbers 57-61. The firm was formerly at number 37, was established in 1892 and specialises in importing and distributing high quality artists' papers. Next to R.K. Burt is the Rose and Crown pub and across the road in O'Meara Street is the Roman Catholic Church Most Precious Blood, 1891, built by the prolific R.C. architect: F.A. Walters. The tall brick facade, with its two bells and iron rose window, and the madonna beside the railway bridge are rather astonishing when first encountered in this small side street (there is another F.A. Walters church in Walworth: St. Wilfred in Lorrimore, 1915).

St. Alphege's Church was demolished in the early 1990's, but buildings associated with it still survive in and around RUSHWORTH STREET. We approach this mysterious, secretive locality via Pocock Street, a turning

Above: *The cellars and warehouses of Max Greger Ltd, Great Guildford Street;* from Pictorial World. March 3, 1883; a similar illustrated feature was published in the Illustrated London News. December 2, 1882. 1: Exterior of vaults and warehouses, extending nearly 600 feet. 2: Floor in warehouse containing 8,000 bottles of Carlowitz in cases ready for export. 3: Packing floor. 4: Top floor of warehouse used for empty casks. 5: The interior of one of the bins. 6: A cellarman bottling Carlowitz. 7: The interior of centre cellar, containing hogsheads of Carlowitz. 8: Cellar boys labelling bottles of Carlowitz. 9: The interior of cellar, showing the exterior of bins, holding 25,000 dozen of bottled wine. 10: End of cellar showing vats each capable of holding 15,000 gallons of wine. The one on the right gained the prize in the Paris Exhibition of 1867, the one next to it was erected in honour of the visit of

off Blackfriars Road. John Rushworth was a seventeenth century lawyer and historian, and spent the last years of his life in the King's Bench Prison. The Pocock's were a local family. In Pocock Street, opposite Pakeman House, City Corporation block of 1938-39, is the eccentric St. Alphege's Clergy House, built in 1910, architect: William Bucknall, with a mixture of Gothic, Georgian and Arts and Crafts styles. The chaplain of the South Bank University is currently in residence here. The church hall extends from Rushworth Street to King's Bench Street; built in 1931 it is occupied by theatrical costume makers and hirers Academy Costumes, and the congregation from the old church. Running parallel to King's Bench Street is Glasshill Street (a reference to the many glass works in nineteenth century Southwark), and here, tucked away, just beneath the railway viaduct, we find the 1820 Drapers Almshouses. Returning to Rushworth Street we find the former Convent of the Reparation, built in 1912 in a neo-Georgian style, architect: Walter Tapper, and now in private residential use. The Ripley and Merrow Buildings are former LCC flats, built 1896-97, architect: A.M. Philips; one hundred years on, with their chimneyed facades, they have considerable charm; grouped around an inner courtyard they rise to only three storeys. A short distance away are two more similar blocks, Albury and Clandon Buildings in Silex and Boyfield Streets; their balconies look out on the street, and surrounded by twentieth century developments, they have a comparable charm and quaintness. Straying away from this locality, we may pass down Pocock Street to the Sawyer Street junction where we encounter the modern, sprawling, low rise Crown Court; we may well shudder with dismay and anxiety, and recall with distinct pleasure the intimate domesticity of the buildings we have just left.

To the east of the southern end of Borough High Street are Tabard Street and Great Dover Street.
TABARD STREET was previously Kent Street (upper end of what is now Old Kent Road), and renamed in 1877 to commemorate the Tabard Inn of Chaucerian fame. At its uppermost end is the community organisation Charterhouse in Southwark, founded in 1885 by former pupils of Charterhouse School. The present day building dates from 1935. Its mission church St Hugh's is at 32 Crosby Row (off Long Lane), where a variety of community projects are also based. Close by in Tabard Street are the headquarters of the Carr-Gomm Society, providing housing for socially disadvantaged people, and established by Richard Carr-Gomm, great-great nephew of Sir William Maynard Gomm, a nineteenth century Lord of the Manor of Rotherhithe. Across the road are the former premises of paper merchants Thom & Cook Ltd, including the distinctive tower of former hardware merchants, tinplaters and japanners Harding & Sons. Progressing further down the street we encounter the large housing block Tabard Gardens, an LCC estate opened in 1916 (housing 2,450 people), with later extensions.

GREAT DOVER STREET runs parallel to Tabard Street and dates from the early nineteenth century when it was constructed as a by-pass. This is a street of large pubs, horrendous office blocks, ugly council housing and a gigantic former engineering works. Babcock Engineering left their 1891 premises at number 165 in the 1980s and the building is now being converted for residential use. The two Victorian pubs the Dover Castle and the Roebuck also bring character to the street. The Dover Castle, 1890, has a pinnacled turret, and is wrapped around with ivy in window boxes and hanging baskets, and street level seating. One can sit here and contemplate the conflicting brutalism of office blocks nearby, such as those at numbers 190 and 200, and the elegance of the eighteenth century St George the Martyr, with its commanding spire, its urns, balustrade and angelic faces.

We can also admire St George's from MARSHALSEA ROAD: a road commemorating the Marshalsea Prison, of Dickens' Little Dorrit fame. One can pass through this road without noticing anything at all, perhaps. The Peabody blocks, Douglas Buildings, in Mint Street, Ilfracombe Buildings in the centre and Monarch Flats are set back, angled so as to give greater prominence to the church at the junction to the east. An interesting nineteenth century terrace can be noted by the Weller Street turning overlooking the site of the former Mint Street workhouse, now grassed over. Modern day organisations are also here: physical therapies are offered by the Dave Prowse Exercise Advice Centre, and close by is the British Association of Occupational Therapists; number 14, a rounded block is dated 1888 high up. Text Systems PLC is at Text House, a large five storey block, and across the road is the Docklands Enterprise Centre.

As we wander the side streets of Southwark, we may discover to our delight several intimate dwelling places from the end of the last century which result from the initiatives of Octavia Hill (1836-1912). She was a pioneer in the conservation and creation of open spaces (leading to the establishment of the National Trust), in housing reform and in bridging the social gulf between the rich and the poor. Today, the Octavia Hill Housing Trust looks after some 1300 homes, and Southwark is fortunate to be the location for several projects designed by Elijah Hoole (architect of Toynbee Hall in the East End): Redcross Cottages and gardens, 1887, set back in

Above: *The northern end of Tabard Street*, with its distinctive Harding & Sons facade.

Above: *Ripley and Merrow Buildings in Rushworth Street*; the old convent building can be glimpsed on the extreme left.

Above: *Tower of Holy Trinity*, Trinity Church Square, 1823-24, architect: F. Bedford; the view is from Brockham Street south of Trinity Street. Converted 1973-75 into a rehearsal and recording centre, Henry Wood Hall.

Above: *The Roebuck pub* stands with this impressive street corner facade at the junction of Great Dover Street with Trinity Street.

Above: *Mint Street: view looking westward*; water-colour, 1840, by T.H. Shepherd; Courtesy: Trustees of the British Museum. Mint Street commemorates Mint Way, part of the estate of the Duke of Suffolk, where Henry VIII had a mint. Another view of Mint Street, looking towards Borough High Street, 1853, is reproduced in the Borough High Street chapter.

Above: *Lant Street*, a drawing by A.D. M'Cormick, from the English Illustrated Magazine, 1888.

Above: *Lant Street*, a drawing by Blanchard, 1920, from *Some Acco the Southwark Diocese*, by the Bisl Woolwich, South London Church 1928.

ove: *A pleasant prospect amidst Southwark's crowded streets*: Redcross Hall and
tages, Redcross Street; from Southwark Annual, 1902. Courtesy: Southwark Local
dies Library.

Opposite: *The Redcross Hall*, architect:
Mr E. Hoole, from the Builder, November
9, 1889. The article also features Gable
Cottages (with full page illustration). The
hall was decorated with murals by Walter
Crane and to the left is that depicting
local heroine Alice Ayre who saved the
children in her charge during a fire,
while dying herself as she tried to escape.
The Southwark Annual writes of the hall:
'The hall is commodious and pleasant
and is constantly at the service of the
people. On Saturday afternoons during
the winter it is thrown open as a sort of
drawing room for grown-up people,
flowers, evergreens, magazines and
photographs and Indian draperies make it
cheerful. Music is provided. The room is
arranged with separate small tables, and
people enter and leave at their will. Tea is
supplied at a small charge. Every week,
besides the entertainments (dramatic or
musical) the hall is used for drill for
cadets, and the club-room for violin,
singing and carving classes. The garden,
besides being open to the public, is used
in conjunction with the hall for a May
festival for children, a flower show of
plants cultivated by working people in
Southwark, and for music'.

REDCROSS WAY, with Whitecross Cottages, 1890 behind in AYRES STREET; and Gable Cottages, 1889, tucked away in Sudrey Street (formerly Little Suffolk Street), a turning of Great Suffolk Street. In SAWYER STREET we find Whitehall Houses, much less interesting, a small block of flats of 1889, architect: L. Ambler, built for the Countess of Selbourne, one of Octavia Hill's associates.

The cottages reassert the importance of small scale housing with quirky design and detail where human individuality and human needs are paramount, and seem to transport us to a gentler, more civilised age; indeed we can be quite startled when we first encounter these cottages, so unprepared are we for them by the surrounding environment. By way of contrast, if we go to the far end of Redcross Way, beyond Southwark Street we will find Cromwell Flats, erected in 1864 by the Improved Industrial Dwellings Company.

LANT STREET is named after Thomas Lant, and was laid out in 1770 after his death. It was he who began the building development of the former Suffolk Palace estate in 1702. It is a street with Dickens' Associations: young Dickens lodged here when his parents were in the Marshalsea Debtors Prison, and Pickwick Papers contains a description of the obscurity of the street and its neighbourhood.

Today, it is a street of pubs, old warehouses, school and church buildings, and many decades later appears to be a more thriving locality; the Waterloo Wine Company now owns the old cork warehouse shown in the Builder engraving; next door is a studio and residential block, and then come the offices of the Daily Jang newspaper. Opposite is the Gladstone Arms pub with two well-painted portraits on the walls outside. Further down is the Charles Dickens School, an old School Board building, formerly Lant Street School, erected in 1877 and enlarged in 1901. It has five street level gables, and a long strip of wrought iron railing in front. Further on is the old Prince of Wales pub, and beyond St Michael's church and hall, now used by the New Life Gospel Church. Opposite is an old commercial complex, of varying dates, renovated in the mid 1980's by Tim Wood, the present owner and an architect, and now housing the service-type organisations and enterprises we associate with regenerated London: the National Listening Library, El Vergel, a delicatessen, and in between offices of designers, photographers, architects and consulting engineers. Thomas Birkett had a flourishing forge here from the late nineteenth century until World War II and the name 'Suthwark Forge' has been preserved on the wall.

As I strayed home one autumn evening, I found myself wondering yet again about the world we are living in today, and where on earth I belonged in it. An Aikido class from Morley College was going on in the church hall: men and girls squatting on mats in their white judo kit. Suddenly, a figure came looming towards me. Well-spoken, he said he was Keith from Adelaide in Australia. I knew at once that he was accosting me for money. He held out his hand, standing there outside the Charles Dickens School.

Back in Borough High Street, late shift city workers were returning home, receiving long distance calls from people they will never meet, they spoke into their mobile phones as they walked; marathoned, boxercised, cases full of faxes, their thoughts focused only on that fat money bag, they trotted away down towards Elephant & Castle. But, supposing at this moment a sedan chair carried by two baseball-capped dwarves should suddenly appear from a side street, and make off across the road? Did such a thought occur to David Fried as he was designing the drawing on the cover of this publication? A memory of Hogarth's rake on his progress down towards madness and damnation? A vision of future Southwark, when walking the streets courts danger and disaster? Countless strange people pass us by everyday on the streets of London, never to be seen again. This is a city beyond all comprehension ...

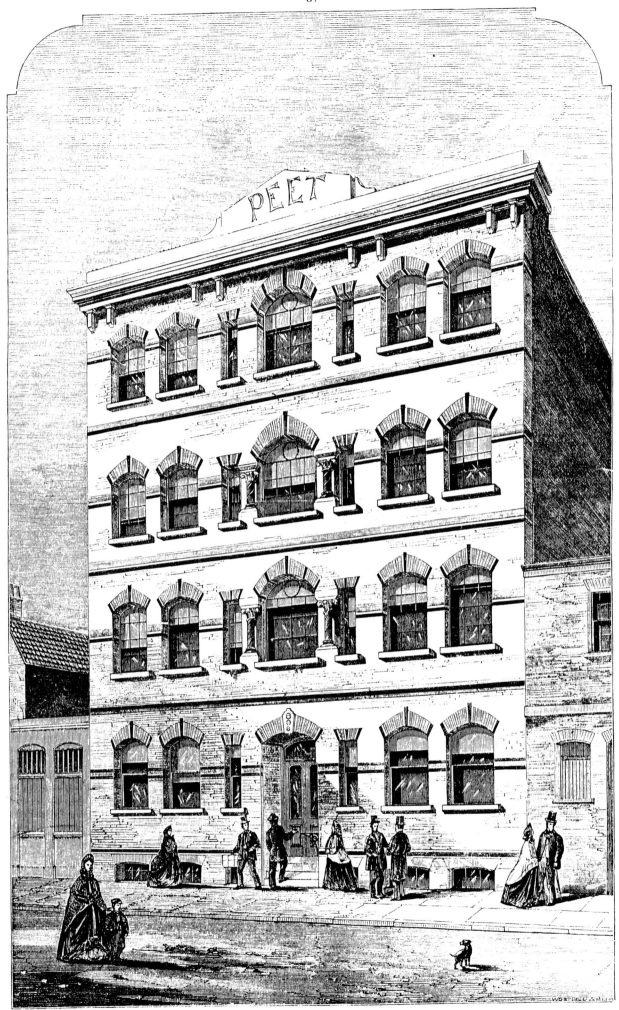

Above: *Cork warehouse, Lant Street, Southwark*; architect: Joseph S. Moye; from the Builder, February 2, 1867. This warehouse, built for Mr Thomas Peet, still stands and currently houses the Waterloo Wine Company.

HUSHED EXPECTANCY: The private worlds of Merrick and Trinity Church Squares

We stumble into this region at the top end of Trinity Square and cannot quite understand where we are: are we somewhere in Bloomsbury? Is this a square somewhere in Islington? Have we gone back in time some 150 years? Everything here is silent and still, as if the residents here know a great deal which they do not wish to disclose. You must stroll around Merrick Square stealthily, because you are not really meant to be here at all; yet curtains are often open at windows; inside you might observe rooms with elegant mirrors, see a sculptured horse on one window ledge, see framed prints on walls, dining tables and chairs laid out for social gatherings, bookcases, pianos; here are all the obligatory trappings of the cultured English middle classes; all proclaim: we have taste, we are educated, we are in the know.

In Trinity Church Square a still greater mystery and secrecy prevail: a few tall bookcases can be seen on upper floors, but ground floors give us few hints as to what happens here; but pianos can sometimes be heard here; here in this place of hushed expectancy, at dusk, as the blackbirds sing in the anxieties of the night, the ecstatic, yet supplicating chordal hymn melody of Schubert's very last piano sonata, written in 1828, might be altogether appropriate for this square laid out 1824-32; this music, expressing too the distant rumbling of trains, the hammer blows of advancing industrialisation, and the desperation of a short life dedicated to inspired poetic beauty almost at its end, seems made for private performance in places like Merrick and Trinity Church Squares; but we are really trespassing here, and must cross the road into less private worlds – the old LCC estate Tabard Gardens and the 1960's blocks: at Dorking and Godstone Houses, the date 1965 is commemorated in stone over the entrances; that is the date when time must have stopped for the residents here.

Lying dangerously close to the time warp of the squares with all their academia and culture is the world of the have-nots: no one cares about those who can see no future for themselves in today's world, those who feel deprived of any kind of stake in today's society. Black youths shout at one another with horrible aggression on the football pitch; an old guy you see walking his alsation dog around here told me that a girl was raped here, someone was murdered.

Above: *Merrick Square*, water-colour, 1963, by Dorothy Mills. Courtesy: South London Gallery. The square was built about 1856 and preserves the memory of Christopher Merrick who gave land to Trinity House in 1661. You can see the arms of Trinity House on a wall in Trinity Street. Brian Williams, a Southwark artist, has also painted this subject.

IN THE LAND OF PHILANTHROPY: Around St George's Circus

Many roads radiate out from Elephant & Castle. If we were seeking one for a quiet Sunday afternoon's stroll, we might choose perhaps St George's Road, and its adjacent streets and square. The dominating building at the northern end is St George's Roman Catholic Cathedral; this gaunt, severe looking building, without tower, is a post World War II rebuilding, designed by Romilly Craze and completed in 1958. The first building was designed by A.W. Pugin, and built between 1841 and 1848. Even if we do not count ourselves amongst the faithful, it is worth penetrating this edifice to see the few nineteenth century survivals: the two effigies to the left of the alt r: Rev. Thomas Provost Doyle, priest at the old church in London Road, known for many years as the Belgian Chapel, initiated the new cathedral; angels guard over Father Doyle; Archbishop Amigo (1864-1949) has none. He was bishop and then Archbishop of Southwark from 1904 to 1949, and is also commemorated in the 1940 Archbishop Amigo Hall to the right of the cathedral entrance. The Knill Chantry built 1856-57 is especially beautiful, with its delicate carvings of birds and angels, and commemorates the relatives of Pugin's third wife, designed by his son E.W. Pugin. Adjacent is the Blessed Sacrament Chapel which has original Pugin fittings, and a majestic gate. To the right of the altar is the chapel of St Peter and the English Martyrs, and in the Lady Chapel there is a small Flemish statue of virgin and child, probably about 1725. Edward Petre was a wealthy landowner, especially concerned about the catholic poor and he gave considerable money for the building of the first cathedral; he is commemorated in the Petre Chantry of 1848-49; photographs and biographical notes are attached to the wall. As we stroll away, the words of a priest officiating at a baptism ceremony booming out over a loudspeaker, we should pause to look at the exhibition showing many photographs of war-time damage and rebuilding, and a display on Pugin and his building. As we pass out into the sunlight, we might find ourselves brooding on the brutality and wanton violence of our own century, and if we have any kind of conscience, may well interrogate ourselves as to our part in it.

Opposite the cathedral buildings in St George's Road at numbers 105-145 is a long terrace of 1842 and an earlier terrace of 1794 at numbers 63-83. Lambeth Road crosses St George's Road and seeking diversion from the solemnity of the cathedral we will enjoy the mural of local scenes by Lynette Lombard and Vincent Milne on the wall of the 1879 St George's pub (currently called the Zanzi Bar). We can inspect the celebrated obelisk across the road, have a snack and wander in the grounds at the Imperial War Museum, observe the local youths ridding their aggression on their footballs, and look across to the Victorian Notre Dame School and Convent, with a large rear building of 1938, and the redundant St Jude's Church.

If we cross over the large play area behind the museum we come to Charlotte Sharman School, the largest block is dated 1884, another is dated 1893; the smaller, gabled buildings are earlier. We have come to West Square: a private, middle class enclave; the residents chose to celebrate its bicentenary by planting a small tree at its centre in September 1991, together with a sundial/bird bath. One wonders whether the neighbours around here ever get round to talking to one another that much. Jen Parker's etching suggests that here, as in countless other places, the very English problem of how to communicate prevails: either we are beset by longing and loneliness, or else we bury ourselves in the written word, blocking out all human contact. The cat and dog she has depicted have very different concerns. The school reminds us of a Victorian lady philanthropist Charlotte Sharman who founded an orphanage nearby in Astral Street. You can read her biography in the book by Marguerite Williams: *Charlotte Sharman: the romance of a great faith*, Religious Tract Society, 1930. Her institutional looking building in Austral Street later became the All Saints Hospital, and is today an annexe of the Imperial War Museum. At the bottom of the street, to the left, adjoining Brook Drive, is an unusual, nineteenth century pub, the Two Eagles, with an attractive sign, and four stone eagles high up on the gables. Nearby is another middle class enclave: Walcot Square is smaller, more regimented, and when I was there felt weighed down by the ennui of a hot August afternoon; but we are now in the London Borough of Lambeth. Turning back into St George's Road, we find another grandiose pub, the Prince of Wales, and close by St George's Buildings, 1900, architects Waring and Nicholson; a large block, Hayles Buildings, is in Elliotts Row, dating from 1890, and its later extension from 1902 similar in style to St George's Buildings.

We can depart from St George's Road feeling that there may still be some hope for civilised living, even if its outward expression is a certain monotony, a certain gravity, and a very English sense of silence.

BOROUGH ROAD leads out of St George's Circus into Borough High Street at the point where the latter turns into Newington Causeway. Laid out in the 1750's, it continues on the other side of St George's Circus as Westminster Bridge Road. In Borough Road the anguish of the High Street evaporates. The buildings here are both grandiose and intimate at the same time, and seem to achieve a kind of high-minded yet contented

Above: *Special staircase*; from an illustrated article in Illustrated London News, December 17, 1892 on the occasion of the opening of the new eye hospital.

Above: The terracotta relief carving on the central gable of the *old library in Borough Road*; note the art nouveau flourishes. A panel depicting the motto 'Truth holding the mirror up to Nature' is on the western gable.

Above: *The Royal London Ophthalmic Hospital*: from Southwark Annual, 1896; Courtesy: Southwark Local Studies Library. An engraving showing the St George's Circus site, with the obelisk and its four lamps, and the Blind School on the left side corner. The hospital was built 1890-92, architect: Keith D. Young, and replaced one hundred years later by the present-day student block McLaren House. There are plans to return the obelisk to its original site (Southwark News, January 17, 1997). An unusual engraving in the Illustrated London News, February 17, 1849, shows the Davies' fire escape of the Royal Society for Protection of Life from Fire at the obelisk.

quietness: this is, after all, South Bank University land. On the corner of St George's Square, next to the Duke of Clarence pub, we note the Obelisk Dairy, dating back to 1810, now a sandwich bar. The obelisk stood in the centre of St George's Circus from 1771 until 1905 and then was moved to St George's Road.

Progressing up the other side of the road we are struck by the relief carvings on the old public library of 1898. Then comes Caxton House, part of South Bank University, and then the old LCC block Murphy House, 1899, also with interesting decoration. Behind are other LCC blocks: Murray, Hunter and Gardiner Buildings, of the same period. A grandiose pub the Bridge House (the sign shows a countryside scene), rebuilt in 1894 comes next, and reminds us of the City of London's Bridge House Estates in Southwark which provide income for the maintenance of London, Southwark, Blackfriars and Tower Bridges. The new housing complex on the western side of the railway bridge is a Gateway Project scheme and aims to provide accommodation for young people, linked with training (provided by the Grand Metropolitan Trust in a centre in Lancaster Street). The Look Ahead Housing Association is involved with the letting of the accommodation. The architects Levitt Bernstein have produced an attractive and interesting building, completed in September 1993. Its 'cut-out' curved blue roof, strips of red brickwork and curving balconies achieve a building style which seems to consider people who will actually live there. The semi-wild garden in the square behind, the fruit cake sculpture by Tim Shutter, and the bicycle shelter are landscape features which one does not immediately associate with 1980's docklands architecture. The new Learning Resources Centre of the South Bank University, across the road in Keyworth Street, conveys a more impersonal atmosphere with its large ground floor windows; the student union building with its shopping mall and bank lies behind.

On the other side of the railway bridge is another large pub the Goose and Firkin, and next to it an old factory of about 1889 with extraordinary, palatial dimensions: five storeyed and with 15 bays, the former premises of blacking manufacturers Day and Martin, and now offices of the International Transport Workers Organisation. After these grandiose, yet friendly buildings, we can sink into the quiet domesticity of the Scovell Estate, built in 1978, with its low rise terraces and tiny back gardens, its potted shrubs, rose bushes and hanging baskets. Built on the site of Queen's Buildings, a Victorian block, the Kings Bench prison was here from 1758 until the 1860's. The attractive four storeyed Ship pub is on the corner.

On the other side of Borough Road we will note the chapel at number 82, now a Deeper Life Bible Church, a branch of Barclays in an eccentric, church-like Edwardian building, originally the South London Institute for the Blind, 1906, architect: C. Ashby Lean, and opposite the Bridge House pub the old Borough Polytechnic building, 1930, architect: Le Maître. As we wander the streets of Southwark, we will often notice mottoes on buildings: here in Borough Road, the educational powers that be urge us to 'Do it with thy might'.

WESTMINSTER BRIDGE ROAD is on the other side of St George's Circus. The glass and brick building at number one is occupied by architects Douglas, Marriott, Worby and Robinson, who designed the building, erected in 1974. They were previously at number five, an old school building, now a 'multi-purpose resource centre', a base for organisations such as the Confederation of Indian Organisations, the Greater London Translation Unit, the Feminist Library, the London School of Law, and the Standing Conference of Ethnic Minority Senior Citizens. Further down the road at number 45 are offices of the Peabody Trust, and opposite The Chandlery comprising offices, studios and workshops in the former Webber Row School, an early E.R. Robson board school of 1876, enlarged in 1884 and later in 1896. We note the characteristic plaques, including one showing a vase of sunflowers. Beyond lies Morley College and its art gallery and the massive tower of Christ Church, the surviving part of the church built in 1873, architects: H.J. Paull and Alfred Bickerdike.

Above: *View of the Royal Circus near the Obelisk in St George's Fields.* Courtesy: Southwark Local Studies Library. An engraving of about 1790 showing the first building of what was later known as Surrey Theatre. It was opened in 1782 by Charles Hughes, one of Astley's horsemen, and Charles Dibden, song-writer, at the southern end of Blackfriars Road; rebuilt in 1809 after fires, it was demolished in 1934 for an extension to the Royal Eye Hospital. It is recorded in a number of eighteenth and nineteenth century engravings: Laurie and Whittle's 1812 engraving (reproduced in LBS' *Scenes from the Past* series); engravings by Wise published by Robert Wilkinson in 1814, and by Dale after Shepherd, 1828, published by Jones & Coin, and an interior view aquatint by Pugin and Richardson, published by Ackermann.

Above: *Magdalen Hospital, for the reception and training of penitent prostitutes*; Courtesy: Southwark Local Studies Library eighteenth century engraving contrasting with the twilight romance of the Royal Circus, next to which it was situated from 1772 unt when it moved to Streatham and the site taken over by Peabody Square. The institution was established in Whitechapel in 1758.

Above: *A madonna beside a railway bridge*, and the street facade of the RC Church Most Precious Blood, in O'Meara Street.

Above: A more worldly object of contemplation: *a fruit cake sculpture, by Tim Shutter* in the semi-wild garden in King James' Street behind the Gateway Project building in Borough Road.

Above, below and opposite: Lithographs by. T. Way from the 10th, 1883 Annual report of *St Alphege's Church, Lancaster Street*. Courtesy: Southwark Local Studies Library. This church, built 1880-82, architect: R. Willey, was demolished in the early 1990's. Buildings associated with it, the clergy house, mission hall, and convent still stand in Rushworth Street nearby.

Above: *Tower of the School for the Indigent Blind*; from the Penny Magazine, November 30, 1838. The school was founded in 1799, the first of its kind in England and occupied premises at the Lambeth and London Roads junction from 1834 until the beginning of the twentieth century when it moved to Leatherhead.

Opposite: *Clock tower, St George's Circus*; from Southwark Annual, 1906. Courtesy: Southwark Local Studies Library. Erected in 1907, replacing the obelisk, and removed in 1937.

Below: *The Freemason's Charity School for Female Children in St George's Fields*; drawn and engraved by S. Rawle, 1801. Courtesy: Southwark Local Studies Library. The charity was founded in 1788, and the building above erected in 1793. It was situated on the northern side of Westminster Bridge Road. Another charitable school nearby was that of the Philanthropic Society for children of parents in prison.

Above: *Public Library, Borough Road*; from the London Argus, February 11, 1899; designed by C.J. Phipps, with A. Bloomfield Jackson, it closed as a library recently, and is now used by the South Bank University Day Nursery. The street scene is especially charming.

Above: *British and Foreign Schools Society and School, Borough Road*; from the Illustrated London News, May 20, 1843. The above replaced an earlier building (engraved and published for the society by F. Warr). The 1843 building became part of the Borough Polytechnic in 1890. Joseph Lancaster started his first school in Borough Road in 1798 (Joseph Lancaster School of today is in Harper Road), and the society for the training of teachers was established in 1805. Unlike the National Society it did not believe in the teaching of church catechism.

98

Above: *New Bethlehem Hospital, St George's Fields*; drawn by T.H. Shepherd, engraved by J. Tingle. Bethlehem Royal Hospital for the mentally ill can trace its origins to the fourteenth century. It moved from its palatial building in Moorfields in the city to the new building, above, designed by James Lewis in 1815. The copper dome we see today dates from 1844. The Imperial War Museum took over the building's central block in 1936, the side wings being demolished and the hospital moved to Beckenham in 1930. A historical account of the hospital was written by the archivist Patricia Allderidge in 1976.

Above: *St Jude's Church*; from the Southwark Annual, 1 Courtesy: Southwark Local Studies Library. This church in George's Road, built 1879, architect: W.J.H. Leverton, is disused, but St Jude's School in Colnbrook Street on the left operates.

Above: A lino-cut based on the *Imperial War Museum*, by Stephen Mumberson, 1991. Part of the Berlin wall stands to the left of the entrance. Two side wings above the central exhibition hall house a selection of work from the museum's extensive art collection.

Above: *The mob destroying and setting fire to the King's Bench Prison and House of Correction in St George's Fields*, published in 1780 by Fielding and Walker. St George's Fields, a large open space which stretched from near St George the Martyr Church to the area around present-day St George's Circus, is remembered historically as the gathering place in 1780 for the Protestant Association's demonstration against pro-catholic legislation, stimulating the Gordon riots. Courtesy: Southwark Local Studies Library.

IN THE LAND OF THE PINK ELEPHANT

If you are a South Londoner, it is hard to avoid the Land of the Pink Elephant: Elephant & Castle is a terminus for routes going in all directions – you pass through here to get to diverse South London locations; you get many bus numbers here; you come here to get to Morley College, or Waterloo, and across the bridge to Holborn. A place to flee from, some would say, choked with people and traffic all day long, who would want to linger here? some would say. In Southwark Local Studies Library you can inspect photographs of the landscape as it was before and after the clearance began in 1956; you can study the dismay of local people standing outside the underground station as familiar sites vanished under the bulldozer; but things change with the times, and in the 1960's a new landscape was created which has now seeped into the consciousness of many a Londoner; with its upgrading and revamping in recent years, it conveys a kind of noisy energy, a kind of vibrancy, full of chaos and crazy turmoil.

You may come here for the shops, full of all kinds of goods: for a belt for your trousers, a bed to sleep on, or a new pair of shoes. There are more shops here than you might think: rambling second-hand bookshops, a pipe and smoking shop, Asian and black arts and crafts shops ... business students might sit in the cafés here and write celebrations today of the joys of capitalism, art students might come to study the diversity of humanity seen through a glass window, write a project on the 24 underground murals by David Bratby and Denise Cook celebrating Southwark life, past and present, unveiled in 1993; study the architecture of Erno Goldfinger (Alexander House, 1962-67; currently being repainted for conversion into flats), and find excitement in the obsessional piling up of geometric shapes, or if feeling light-hearted, might go around photographing all the pink elephants they can find, seeing in the elephant a symbol for every plodding Londoner weighed down with his burden of worries. On Sundays the faithful make a pilgrimage here to attend services at the Metropolitan Tabernacle: heads bent low, this is where many young Christian people feel they have found a haven and a spiritual home.

For solitary people, this can be a dreadful place, to be sure. Standing on the upper storey gallery of the shopping centre as the home-going stampede gathers pace, one can search and search in this crowd of scurrying people for just one friendly face and find no one; endless little bundles of destiny all propelling themselves forward. In London most people think only about themselves, seek only to establish a clear path for themselves in the jungle of existence in this monstrous capital city; but driven in on themselves with so much screen-gazing, workers of today seem more isolated than ever before, feel within themselves a raging alienation and a longing for vicarious violence which they find hard to fully comprehend. Everyone carries his little pack of stuff: look at the diversity of the bags everyone is carrying around: shoulder bags, brief cases, executive cases, sports bags of all sizes, demon runners charging home with their clothes in ruck sacks, plastic bags, bags containing personal computers which crooks could so easily grab and run off with; everywhere you look people are carrying something around: their possessions of identity, their preoccupations of the moment.

Today, and tomorrow, and the next day and the next, the desperate observer might say, the rat race of the big city will never end; everyone is after the money bag dangling there before one's very eyes; and so jerked this way and that, we all live in a land of anxiety and confusion, and cannot say what is going to happen to us next. The money bag ... after the money bag ... you've got to get money to live, every Londoner will say.

Thus thinks this solitary observer one afternoon in the Land of the Pink Elephant, before going home to Bermondsey and a tub of Burgundy cherry ice cream, and a symphony by Gustav Mahler.

Returning to the Elephant: Subway murals

Scurrying down the various tunnels of the Elephant & Castle subway, intent on our exit and destination, it is possible that we may be conscious of brightly painted tiles flickering on the edges of our vision. On days when we are less harassed and preoccupied, we may well stop and have a look. Here, we may conclude, is something rather splendid, interesting and attractive which we can show off to visitors and friends from other parts.

The twenty-four murals by David Bratby and Denise Cook are part of a major revamping and transformation programme initiated by Southwark Council, involving new entrances, lighting, and retiling, new paving, and tree planting during the early 1990's. One subway at the Newington Butts end has been left in its original state, perhaps intentionally, for people to contrast the two? The mural subjects by Denise Cook (extending to several walls) are at the New Kent Road entrance: Victorian street scenes showing strips of shops and buildings, individuals and groups, and portraits of Southwark personalities, and two views of the Elephant & Castle pub, pre-1818, and 1898-1959; at the Elephant & Castle entrance (opposite the main entrance to the

101

Above: *Sketched from life in the Metropolitan Tabernacle*, June 7, 1891; Mr Spurgeon's last sermon; from Pictorial World, February 6, 1892, on the occasion of his death. The article also illustrates the Stockwell orphanage (where a fine memorial to him was erected), and the almshouses attached to the Tabernacle. He was born in 1834 and commenced preaching when a teenager. In the drawing shown, with its emptying hour glass, he ponders, perhaps, on the ultimate success of his life's work. He is buried at West Norwood Cemetery beneath a massive sarcophagus.

Opposite: A water-colour, c. 1950 by David T. Rose; Courtesy: South London Gallery; shows dome of the deep lying underground station. The City and South London Line (now the Northern Line) opened in 1890.

shopping centre) there are underwater and jungle scenes. The others, by David Bratby, are at the entrances in St George's Road, London Road and Newington Causeway. Sixteen are sited at the later two entrances, and may have been placed here intentionally with the student population from the South Bank University nearby in mind; but they seem calculated to appeal to all sections of the community, young and old. Local people, for example, feature in paintings adapting ideas from Van Gogh (he lived at Ivy Cottage, 395 Kennington Road in 1874), Charlie Chaplin (street and restaurant scenes), and Hogarth (an enigmatic scene showing children, adapting, apparently Hogarth's Southwark Fair). There are dramatic views of Surrey Docks (figures handling timber and rope at each corner), the Trocadero Cinema (together with a number 68 bus), a Shakespeare performance at the George Inn, and an updated multi-racial scene from Little Dorrit, interiors of the 1930's and 1950's (also multi-racial), and paintings of two entertainments at Surrey Gardens (Assault on Gibraltar, showing also scenes from the gardens, and Vesuvius erupting). Annual summer festivals in Southwark today are recreated in four carefully observed paintings with diverse human interest. At the St George's Road entrance one finds paintings celebrating the Afro-Asian community in particular with carnival scenes: dancing from Trinidad, a Vietnamese-Chinese dragon dance, and an elephant procession from Sri Lanka (seven elephants are shown).

All these carefully planned and brilliantly executed murals are, on reflection, highly successful, perhaps a model for many other central urban areas where an injection of vitality and optimism is needed. Southwark people should be rightly proud of the work of David Bratby and Denise Cook, and extend to them their heartfelt thanks. The Southwark Council was quite right to feature their work in their glossy booklet *The Elephant*, but a number of the photographs give truncated versions of the paintings, and paintings of this scale, and in a subway location, need to be experienced on site.

Above: *Elephant Buildings, Newington Butts*, main premises of Edward Harris Rabbits, boot and shoe maker, est. 1846; from an 1861 trade bill. There were also eleven branch establishments throughout London, including four in South East London. The above building later became the South London Repository. The London School of Printing stands on the site today. Courtesy: Southwark Local Studies Library.

Above: Before the erection of the above, and the tabernacle, the *Fishmongers Almshouses* stood on the site; the above illustration from the Lady's Newspaper, December 9, 1848 shows the building (also known as St Peter's Hospital), erected by the Fishmongers Company in 1615-18. A birds-eye engraving published in The Mirror of Literature, Amusement and Instruction, April 11, 1840 also shows the adjacent range erected in 1719, the bequest of a liveryman James Hulbert. Another small illustration was published in the Illustrated London News, February 17, 1849 and there is a T.H. Shepherd water-colour, c. 1850.

104

Above: *The premises of William Tarn & Co, drapers, mid-nineteenth century. Courtesy: Southwark Local Studies Library. By the end of the century it had developed into a large store with workshops and factories attached. The building in the*

Above: *A visit to the South London Tabernacle: Baptism by immersion;* from Pictorial World, December 4, 1875. The baptistery was situated in a railed-in area beneath the pulpit (see Pictorial World, February 6, 1892). This somewhat dream-like drawing comments perhaps on the willing conformity and submission to authority of those who wish to be initiated into the membership of a church.

Above: A drawing, 1920's, showing the *Bakerloo Line undergr[ound] entrance, with offices of the South London Press newspaper ab[ove]* Courtesy: Southwark Local Studies Library. The paper was fou[nded] by James Henderson, and had its first offices in Red Lion Court[,] Fleet Street. It has been based for many years now in Streatham [.] The Bakerloo line reached the Elephant & Castle in 1906. The a[bove] building still stands, with its original ground floor red glazed [tiles,] somewhat dwarfed today by the Department of Health's Ski[pton] House, behind, opened in 1993.

Opposite: *A famous pub sign re-sited*, outside the canopy entran[ce to] the shopping centre. Behind is the twenty-five-storey tower of [the] 1960's Draper Estate. There has been a pub or tavern with [the] Elephant & Castle name since 1765. The splendid 1898 buildin[g at] the top of Walworth Road had the symbol on its roof top, betw[een] two domes. The present-day pub with this name has a [less] conspicuous symbol, but it appears in different guises here: above [the] subway entrances, as a football at the leisure centre, a floral dis[play] nearby, and becomes a circus performer at the shopping centre (t[here] is a large tiled mural at the New Kent Road entrance). An interes[ting] mural at the entrance to the railway station (black elephant, watc[hing] eyes, Charlie Chaplin), by S. M'Garrity, F. Davies, and S. Bender [is] now gone, replaced in 1997 by a painted colonnaded garden w[ith] scene.

Above: *Interior of the Metropolitan Tabernacle*; from the Builder, May 4, 1861. Published on the occasion of the opening of the new building (see Illustrated London News, April 6, 1861). The facade remains, but the wood panelled interior is modern. The above illustration is probably an unusual depiction of the arrival and gathering of a congregation, and the evocation of a sense of expectancy.

IN AND AROUND NEW KENT ROAD

This is a road and locality which arouses a strange mix of emotions – full of traffic and people going about their business, with buildings both gigantic and small, with take-away food shops and small parks and gardens; this is a place which seems dreadful and soulless, intimate and friendly, threatening and peaceful all at the same time.

One can enjoy, perhaps, perambulating the walkways around the Heygate Estate, but this is a terrifying construction: gigantic slabs containing 1,194 dwellings built between 1970-74; many doorways are protected with iron gates. Can such a dwelling-place give people any sense of pride, any identity, any sense of belonging? Yet here, as elsewhere, indeed anywhere in the world, people contrive to make a little nest for themselves, fill their homes with items of identity, put little knick-knacks on the window ledges for all to see; coming to flats emptied by previous occupants, people quickly turn empty, hollow spaces into shrines dedicated to self-preservation in this gigantic city, in any large city in the world, anywhere. Further up the road is another hugue dwelling-place, but from another era: Driscoll House, built in 1913, was formerly the Ada Lewis Hostel for Women. In 1968 the building was acquired for five million pounds by Mr and Mrs Driscoll, Roman Catholics, who ran many properties in Croydon, housing overseas students and missionaries. Two plaques unveiled in 1991 commemorate the fallen from the Commonwealth and America during the two World Wars.

Less formidable buildings in the road provide contrast: there is a late eighteenth century terrace at numbers 154-170; and another range, dating from 1818-19, can be found in Bartholomew Street near the flyover. A plaque, at number 17 Bartholomew Street, commemorates the architect and artist Sir Ernest George (1839-1922), who was born there. You can see many of his buildings in Streatham. Number 195 is an attractive Victorian building housing offices of Southwark's Family Courts Welfare Service.

Small, attractive parks and gardens can be hunted out and enjoyed around here: Victory Community Park off Balfour Street, the Rockingham Community Park on the corner of Falmouth Road, and the David Copperfield Gardens. Here a memorial was erected by the Dickens Fellowship in 1931: a boy blowing a shell, a reference to an episode in the novel, the plinth informs us; yet several years ago the sculpture was smashed up, mutilated, and a brick left lying around for ages. When we encounter such outrages we know we are living in a very disturbed society.

There are churches around here too: the old St Matthew's Church of 1855, by Henry Jarvis, was demolished in the early 1990's and replaced by a new church and community building nearby in Meadow Row; the new church, 1993, was designed by Hans Haenlein, architects in Hammersmith. The small metal bell tower is an attractive feature, and inside one will find other fittings, all carefully designed: candlestick holders, a stoup, a font, stained glass paintings and icons. Across the road there is the Crossway United Reformed Church replacing an earlier mission church, a cross hanging on a five-line stave, built 1975, architects: Beard, Benett and Wilkins, and opposite in Falmouth Road is a former Welsh chapel, built 1888, now run by the Nigerian Brotherhood of the Cross and Star. With its red entrance doors and brown brickwork, this church looks warm and friendly, and no doubt countless passers-by glimpse its facade as they pass up and down the New Kent Road. At number 81 is the old vicarage of St Matthew's, and number 83 now houses students from the South Bank University.

If we probed ourselves a little further, perhaps we would simply feel an overwhelming sense of dread and boredom in this place, feeling that life does not really add up to anything much at all, want to get back home, shut the door, and try to forget that time has passed, that people have passed away, that we are still here, that the Millennium is on the horizon, that we must go on, still find some way of muddling through the days, living as we do on the edge, alone, forgotten.

Above: *St Saviour and St Olave School for Girls*; from Southwark Annual, 1904. Courtesy: Southwark Local Studies Library. The school was designed by W. Campbell Jones, and is situated at the lower end of New Kent Road. It was opened in 1903 by the Prince and Princess of Wales (photograph in SBR in Old Photographs).

Above: *195 New Kent Road*, a former police station.

Above: *Old houses in Bath Terrace*; a drawing by A.D. M'Cormick, from the English Illustrated Magazine, November 1888. Bath Terrace leads off Harper Road.

Above: Epsom, Welsh chapel, now church of the Brotherhood of the Cross and Star. 1899. Edward Pugh. Architect A.W. Clark. E.

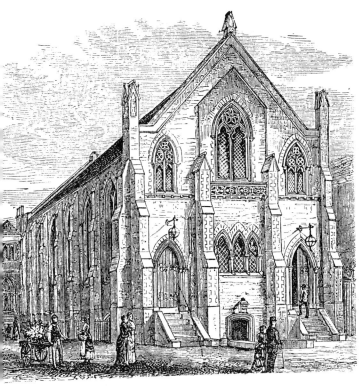

Opposite: *Pilgrim Fathers Memorial Church, Buckenham Square*; from Southwark Annual, 1903. Courtesy: Southwark Local Studies Library. The church traces its origins back to a group of dissenters who formed an independent church in 1592. Its founder members were punished with incarceration and eventually death; others fled to Amsterdam, or sailed with the Mayflower to America in 1620. It found a permanent home in Deadman's Place (now part of Park Street), for about 100 years, moving in 1787 to a new site in Union Street. It moved to Buckenham Square in 1864 and after World War II to a new building in Great Dover Street. The church there was dissolved in 1972 and the building is now administered by the Crossway U.R. Church. Southwark Heritage Association has recently published a leaflet: *Mayflower: American heritage in Southwark and the City*, and there is a booklet *Clink: the story of a forgotten church*, by a former pastor Dennis Godfrey, c. 1966.

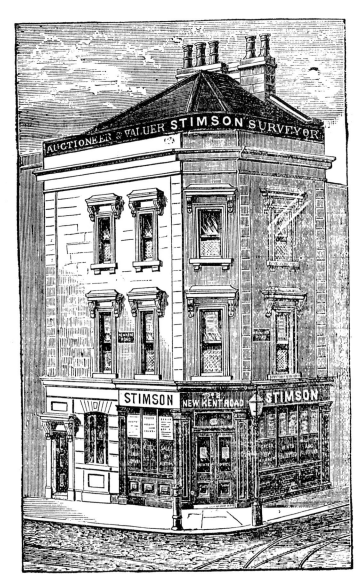

Above: *New bell-tower of St Matthew's Church, Meadow Row*, with Guy's Tower in the background.

Opposite: An illustration from the firm's selected list of properties for sale, June 1880. Courtesy: Southwark Local Studies Library.

112

Above: *Board Schools, Harper Road*, from The Architect, February 14, 1874. Courtesy: Southwark Local Studies Library. The school is now the Joseph Lancaster Primary School. A notice outside proclaims that it is a school where 'learning comes first', and that it believes in 'kindness, good behaviour, honesty, manners, excitement, meeting new people'. Nearby is the Geoffrey Chaucer School with its pentagonal hall and parabolic roof, 1958, architects: Chamberlain, Powell & Son. Harper Road leads past a 1968-71

MAKING SENSE OF OLD KENT ROAD

Imagine you have just come to London, and have moved into a flat or bedsit in the Old Kent Road. This long, ancient road, stretching from Bermondsey to New Cross, could at first reduce anyone to unease and desperation: how to feel at home here, where you simply do not know who you might encounter, how to find friends, how to put down your roots here. Yet London is home for millions; despite its sprawling enormity, we map out our patch both physically and mentally, work out its boundaries, its landmarks, note its re-occurring faces; familiarity brings comfort, the streets wrap themselves around our existences; the shops are full of produce, buses take us in and out, we discover corners where we are safe, establish our haunts and make social contacts; days come and go and it is possible that eventually we find ourselves living in one place for many years. This is what often happens when you come to London.

The Old Kent Road and its side streets can be studied as elsewhere in Southwark for dramatic contrasts and juxtapositions, for the mix of nineteenth and twentieth centuries. Starting from the flyover at the Tower Bridge Road junction there is the old Bacon's School building, 1896, now converted into flats, and then nearby a pub called The World Turned Upside Down (footballs kicking the footballers, a fish catching the fisherman), sandwiched between two blocks Waleran Flats and Kingsley Flats, part of the Peabody Trust Bricklayers Arms Estate. Further on at number 155, the White House might arouse curiosity. Built in 1800, this was home and offices of the architect Michael Searles; he designed the impressive Paragon Crescent for John Rolls in 1788, demolished to make way for the 1898 Paragon School (now a gym) in Searles Road to the west. In 1996 a centre of the Dynamic Gospel Ministries World Outreach, the Chrysolyte Independent Christian School and offices for financial advice were based here. On the other side of the road we might stray into Surrey Square, also a Rolls estate development, and see the surviving long terrace, designed by Michael Searles in 1793-94, notice the large fan-line design on the pediment and the plaque at number 42 recording the birth here of the artist Samuel Palmer (1805-81).

Many shops and businesses throng this end of the Old Kent Road: Churchill's Architectural Salvage specialise in Georgian, Victorian and Edwardian fireplaces; the Miami Health Club has on offer all kinds of physical therapies. More fireplaces and antiques are sold at Blue Mantle Antiques, occupying the old fire station of 1903; two waving mechanical firemen stand in the upper windows. This is an unusual corner of Southwark: on one side of the old 1903 fire station there is the Green Man pub, on the other, beyond a strip of shops, the Thomas à Becket pub, two grandiose nineteenth century buildings. The Thomas à Becket pub, rebuilt 1898, architect: Richard Willcock, is famous for its boxing gym upstairs; established in 1943 its closure was recently announced; the pugilists will no doubt transfer to the Henry Cooper pub further down the road where another gym operates. In Albany Road nearby there is Madhouse Tyres, and across the road the Southernwood Retail Park, opposite Tesco's, with its warehouse structures of Carpet Right, Harvey's, Cur ry's, and Powerhouse.

The entrance to Burgess Park was revamped in 1995, and now there are hanging baskets and three vandal-proof wrought iron Camberwell butterflies to entice us into this expansive open space, with a large lake at its centre. There are more butterflies at the Camberwell Road entrance, near Addington Square. Progressing down the long road, we find turnings which lead to terraces of Georgian housing and nineteenth century churches. At the top end of Oakley Place is the old Methodist chapel, erected in 1874, and on the same side a nice Victorian terrace. There are mysterious, tall, late Georgian houses in Cobourg Road and at its bottom end old St Mark's church, designed by Norman Shaw, and now the New Peckham Mosque. Stuccoed villas in Trafalgar Avenue, Glengall Terrace and Glengall Road, dating from about 1845 hint at a time when living was more civilised and gracious; in houses like these the playing of Mendelssohn pianoforte songs without words might seem appropriate. Glengall Road also has a church: old St Andrew's, with an unusual tower, designed by E. Bassett Keeling in 1865, and now a Celestial Church of Christ (Nigeria). The tower in its restored version has lost its spire (see drawing in ILN, 1866).

At the corner of Trafalgar Avenue and Old Kent Road is the Lord Nelson pub; with its entrance in Trafalgar Avenue, it could easily be missed on a journey down the Old Kent Road. The building dates from the late eighteenth century, and with its two strips of wrought iron, two lamps, and ornamental clock, it conveys a much period charm, charm which one would be hard-pressed to find in the cardboard cut-outs of Wessex House, 1971-74, and the fire station opposite.

Looking at Council housing estates is probably not many people's idea of having fun, but we may like to penetrate Avondale Square, designed by Sir Lancelot Keay, Basil Duckett & Partners for the City Corporation 1958-62. Blocks of varying sizes look down on St Philip's Church in its midst, octagon shaped, designed by N.F. Cachemaille Day in 1963 and replacing the bombed church of 1875; the old vicarage and church hall, c.

Above: *The Lord Nelson pub*, on the corner of Trafalgar Avenue; Lord Nelson's last, fatal battle was at Cape Trafalgar, off Cadiz, on October 21, 1805.

Below: *The Thomas à Becket pub* on the corner of Albany Road, opposite a Tesco's store, commemorating the route of the Canterbury pilgrims to the shrine of Thomas à Becket, appointed Archbishop of Canterbury in 1162, murdered in 1170 and canonized in 1173. A stream and halting spot on the site of the pub was known as St Thomas à Watering. An etching of the bar of the pub by John Hewitt appears in the collection of prints *The New Microcosm of London*, published by Jerry Leese.

Above: The more restrained exterior of the *Rising S* *pub* on the corner of Hillbeck Close, at the New Cr end of Old Kent Road.

1914, survive. Between the church and the church hall there is a small memorial garden: six tablets record names of people you and I have never known. The sculpture by Anthony Weller, commissioned in 1962 of a woman and her dog is a piece of great sensitivity and beauty, facing the mundane shopping precinct across the square.

As we progress further down the road, everything gets both bigger and smaller; we feel we are moving from one borough into another; a place of transition where we are not too sure where we are. The B & Q Supercentre of Olmer Street is a gigantic warehouse store, selling all kinds of DIY and household produce. Comet deals in audio-visual goods and domestic appliances, Halfords in motoring and cycling accessories. Next door to this celebration of practical existence, not wishing to be outdone, is the Tile Kingdom, importers and exporters of fine ceramic tiles.

I was here one hot summer afternoon, not to shop, but to see more Camberwell beauty butterflies. Before they appeared at the two entrances to Burgess Park, they were already here on the facade of North Peckham Civic Centre Library. Adam Kossowski's fine 1965 mosaic mural depicting various periods of history from Romans to the pearlies includes 10 ceramic butterflies on the corner, and inside the library hanging from the ceiling is Brian Kneale's steele sculpture; oh yes, the Schmetterling, said the library assistant, and perhaps the German word is altogether more appropriate for this strange apparition in the library. Another big superstore shed housing Office World and Allied Carpets is across the road. Opposite this twentieth century commercialism is an interesting strip of nineteenth century buildings: the Royal London Insurance building, Christ Church, designed by E. Bassett Keeling, 1868, replacing an earlier church of 1837, with an eccentric tower, and the Southwark Council-run Livesey Museum.

The museum commemorates Sir George Livesey, chairman of the South Metropolitan Gas Company and local philanthropist. The building was originally a library: 'Camberwell Public Library Number 1', and high up on the ornamental cartouche we are reminded 'The word of the Lord endureth for ever'; built 1890, architect: R.P. Whellock. The Livesey Museum is not a museum as such with a permanent collection, but it mounts educational exhibitions and is worth visiting for some interesting and surprising artefacts. To the left as we enter hangs Grace Golding's large oil painting of a teeming river at London Bridge. Outside is a charming courtyard around the remains of part of the library which was bombed and never rebuilt. Attached to the wall you will find a model of the front of a local firm Edgington's, founded in 1805 and famous for its tent, rope and sail making. The business moved from the Old Kent Road in 1967 and the original front is at Woburn Abbey. The most recent acquisition is the statue of Sir George Livesey, sculpted in 1909 by F.W. Pomeroy, donated to the museum with the closure of the gas works in 1996. It is an imposing statue of a man much loved by his employees and stands on an elaborate plinth. In front, hanging from a window, is a large bell, from St Alban's School in Walworth Road. There are other miscellaneous objects scattered about: an Edwardian ice cream barrow, the stonebreaker's 'grill' from Camberwell workhouse, the Newington tollgate, a cattle trough, railings believed to have come from Peckham Manor, and most colourful of all the two mosaics by Thomas Adrian Cook, 1910, from the library further west in Old Kent Road, demolished in 1967, depicting Canterbury pilgrim scenes. This curious corner of Southwark deserves to be cherished and preserved.

In front of the gasworks on the other side of the road (gas holders date from 1867-81) the Holy Fire Revival Ministries operate from nondescript, squat buildings and proclaim 'Our god is a consuming fire'; next door is the London Transit Van Centre. We are in a strange place; to reassure ourselves and escape again into the last century, we can find pleasure in looking at old buildings around here, both detached and terraced: Elizabeth Place, 1844; Doddington Place, 1833, and Doddington Cottages, 1836 are at the top end of Commercial Way; the pub on the corner Drovers is of the same period, and has a panoramic, curving mural. If we strayed into Bird-in-the-Bush Road, leading off Commercial Way, we would pass the old board school of 1893, might enjoy the bird in the bush mural behind the fish and chip shop overlooking the cycling track, and further on be impressed by the towering Our Lady of Sorrows Roman Catholic Church, 1864-66, architect: E.W. Pugin, with its large friary.

Trees in summer can often conceal buildings completely, and from Old Kent Road you probably would miss the old almshouses of the Licensed Victuallers Benevolent Institution, designed by Henry Rose, 1827-33 and now renamed Caroline Gardens and in the care of Southwark Council. This enormous range with its elegant entrance gate commemorating one hundred years of existence in 1927 is even bigger than you might imagine; the Albert wing (as depicted below) is situated at the rear with another garden in front. If we stray a bit further down Asylum Road we can find Clifton Terrace, 1846-52, restored by Southwark Council 1977 and attractive to look at with its modest iron railings, red brick, and green window canopies.

We are now close to the Lewisham border; we can find pleasure in two grandiose pubs: the Rising Sun and the Windsor Hall (recently renamed The Hairy Lemon), and the more intimate, early nineteenth century Carlton Cottages (two semi-detached cottages), with their ammonite capitals. There is another, detached cottage currently boarded up, on the other side of the railway bridge.

Above: The poetic sign (as at January 1997) of the *Rising Sun pub* (799 Old Kent Road).

Above: *A statue of George Thomas Livesey* recently donated to the Livesey Museum. He became company secretary to the South Metropolitan Gas Company in 1871, transformed its fortunes and introduced a profit-sharing scheme.

Above: *A sculpture by Anthony Weller*, commissioned in 1962 for the opening of the new City Corporation estate Avondale Square.

Opposite: *A 'Pearly' family*, depicted by Adam Kossowski, at the end of his mural on the facade of North Peckham Civic Centre. Originally elected by their fellow costermongers to safeguard their rights, their main activity today is collecting for charity. We note their pleading expressions in the scene.

We have come to the end of the journey down the Old Kent Road, more surprising than frightening, perhaps; but it is easy to feel way off the beaten track down here, and it is probably best to catch the bus back to Bermondsey.

Opposite: The former chapel building of the almshouses in the centre of the front range, as shown on the sign of the pub The Asylum Tavern nearby.

bove: An engraving from the Illustrated London News, December 4, 1858. The Albert Wing is named after Prince Albert who laid ιe foundation stone here on June 23, 1858, as he had done for the ladies wing in 1849; the block was completed in 1862. The statue ˙ Prince Albert, unveiled by the Prince of Wales in 1864 in the front garden was moved to the Licensed Victuallers' new home in enham, Bucks, in 1959.

Above: *Asylum for the Deaf and Dumb*; rebuilt in 1886; an engraving from c. 1900. The founder John Townsend (1757-1826) is buried in Bunhill Fields and is commemorated by the primary school bearing his name on the site at the upper end of Old Kent Road. Established in 1792, the first building was erected in 1807, and was illustrated by various engravers (including J. Greig for the Gentleman's Magazine, April 1822). The asylum moved its pupils to Margate in 1903 where there had been a school for deaf children since 1860. There is a memorial to Joseph Watson, the asylum's first teacher in St Mary Magdalene Church, Bermondsey. Building News, June 27, 1886 has a large size engraving of the Old Kent Road premises. Other landmark buildings in Old Kent Road, also now demolished include: Camberwell Baths (near the gas works); Carters (men's outfitters at number 194); depicted by Tina Conway in a lithograph held by the Museum of London, and a water-colour, 1970, by K. Thorpe, held by the South London Gallery; Ben Beber, men's tailor had old premises at number 293 (now site of Tesco's), and are depicted in another lithograph by Tina Conway (also held by Museum of London); they are now across the road at number 288.

Above: *Sidmouth Arms pub, now renamed The Bush Tavern*, on the corner of Bird in Bush Road and Commercial Way.

WANDERING ABOUT IN WALWORTH

Walworth Road may be a place full of shops, a place full of the hurley-burley of daily life as people come and go, buy their provisions and necessities, go about their business; the Walworth district may be full of endless terraces and blocks all looking monotonously the same; yet it is an historic place, once a village with a common and a manor, and the property of Canterbury Cathedral until 1862.

Indeed, people in search of antiquities will come down to Walworth Road, mount the stairs of the public library, to visit the Cuming Museum, opened as long ago as 1906, the bequest of Henry Seyer Cuming (1817-1902), son of Richard Cuming Junior, and brother of Ann Cuming, artist and poet. In the introductory cases you can read the story of Richard Cuming Senior (1736-1801), a tin-plater from Totnes, who found wealth trading in the city of London. There were three children, Richard Cuming Junior (1777-1870), the antiquarian and collector, John Brompton Cuming (1772-1851), artist (and known for his rural views of the locality), and a daughter who died in infancy. They lived at 3 Dean's Row, Walworth Road from 1779, and from 1850 to 1902 the family house was at 63 Kennington Park Road. The bequest consisted of many thousands of items including London material. Henry Cuming for example, collected many objects dug up at building and railway works; he had a special interest in the faking of antiquities too, and cases show the work of the forgers 'Billy and Charley' (William Smith and Charles Eaton), two London mudlarks who had a workshop from 1857 in Rosemary Lane, Tower Hill.

As we start to work our way round the cases, we may be intentionally amused by strange objects, to entice us further on: an ancient Egyptian mummified leg, satin shoes worn by Queen Victoria in 1852, a thermometer in a walnut shell; there is a striking ceramic relief 'The Jews making bricks in Egypt', by local potter George Tinworth (who worked all his life for Doulton's). More curiosities are in the cases showing items from the Lovett collection of London superstitions: a catskin's cure for whooping cough and a lucky charm boot catch our attention. There are the customary cases devoted to periods of history and archaeological finds, two models of Southwark Cathedral, a model of South London Palace and a model of Newington Butts before 1850 by a local wheelwright Robert Alford. There are larger exhibits too: a brown bear, bought by Robert Cuming at the Leverian Museum sale, a milk cart of about 1900 (from Martin Brothers, 89 Walcot Square), a pump from the Marshalsea Prison, used between 1760 and 1820 (and often featuring in the 1987 Little Dorrit film).

It is a strange museum, and we walk out into the present day street feeling just a little time-dazed, finding it momentarily hard to reorientate ourselves back into the late twentieth century: but buildings are at hand to lead us forward: municipal buildings of the former borough of Southwark stand nearby: the old vestry hall, now town hall, of 1866 (with a World War II memorial attached), architect: Jarvis; the library and museum building, 1893, architect: Edward l'Anson; and the Health Services Department building, 1937, architect: P. Stuart, with the motto 'The health of the people is the highest law', and a mother and children sculptured group on the roof-top.

G. Baldwin & Co, health food shop, established as long ago as 1844 is at number 171, and at number 181 there is an indoor market, advertised with a bright fairy-tale painting and the words 'Crazy Prices Kingdom' over the entrance.

Across the road we find the old Manor Place baths, operational from 1898 until 1978. The clock tower is an attractive feature, bringing charm to an area dominated by large, old and new housing estates and a modern police station. Close by we find the 1890's Pullens Estate, heavily, if repetitively, decorated, and with unusual workshop yards behind. Pullens Gardens in Amelia Street is a new park garden, opened in 1994, packed full with plants, shrubs and trees, with both wild and bedded areas, seating, a childrens' play area and lawns: a delightful corner of Walworth. Continuing on down Penton Place we encounter the Giraffe pub: it has two giraffes painted on its walls, as well as one on its sign, and reminds us of the existence here until 1872 of Surrey Gardens (zoo, music hall, pleasure gardens), and the five giraffes who came to the zoo, the first to be seen in England. Retracing our steps, Manor Place leads into Chapter Road and Lorrimer Square. The Jarvis St Paul's church of 1854-56 was replaced in 1955-60 with a new church designed by Woodroffe, Buchanan & Coulter: a large, thrusting building with spiky gables and dormer windows in a copper roof. The walls of the church have small, honeycomb patterned windows, and rise above the ground floor which houses church offices, a youth centre, the London Ecumenical Aids Trust, and the Southwark Crossroads Care Attendant Scheme. Beyond, to the south lies the Brandon Estate: six eighteen-storey towers built 1957-58, with curious roof-top, curved services structures, and five twenty-six-storey towers built in the 1960's. In their midst, on a grass mound, there is a Henry Moore sculpture 'Reclining figure', reminiscent of his work in Stifford Estate in Stepney.

Above: *Vestry Hall, Walworth Road*; from the Builder, May 26, 18 (plan also included). Later became Southwark Town Hall (for the London Borough of Southwark). The building extends down Wan Street to the left and another bay exists to the right; the railings h altered but this impressive facade still remains. Brian Williams' painting of this subject, 1991, emphasises the red brickwork a shows part of the adjacent library.

Opposite: *The clock tower, and chimney of the old Manor Baths*, opened in 1898; closed in 1978; baths for washing swimming. The long facade, with six entrances feels war comparison with the clinical looking 1990's housing block oppos

Returning to the northern end of Walworth Road, and walking into Larcom Street near the municipal buildings, we encounter an altogether more peaceful atmosphere around St John's church, another Henry Jarvis church, built 1859-60. A little further on, in Brandon Street, we find Walter's Close, almshouses built around two courtyards for the Drapers Company in 1961, the original buildings dating from 1642 and situated further north and commemorating John Walter, a clerk to the company. Behind the almshouses is a large Peabody estate, a striking housing contrast. When London finally falls down, perhaps centuries into the future, travellers and academics will come to such places to ponder on the ruins of the distant past, draw and paint them, like our ancestors doing the Grand European Tour. These gigantic blocks have a grandeur which is made more striking by the proximity of the Heygate Estate. When I was there one hot August afternoon, little brown kids scooted about on their mini bikes, played tennis with squashed booze cans, and sprawled in the sun on the hard concrete.

As I was approaching the former Lady Margaret Church in Chatham Street, built 1888-89, architect: Ewan Christian (now part of the Eternal Sacred Order of Cherubim and Seraphim), I was accosted by a young person with a plastic bag who asked me if I spoke English, and then asked me where he could find a church which was open as he desperately needed some money. He had just lost his job as a chef in a hotel in Central London, driven out by an accusation of racial harassment, he told me. He lived in a small bedsit-flat in Camberwell, and had a £200 gas bill to pay and had no money to buy food as his unemployment claim was being assessed. This is the Southwark, or indeed the London of desperation, it could easily be you or me, and it is at such times that the nightmare of London existence becomes far too real, and at such times you know only too well that nobody simply cares.

August in London is the hardest month to survive, perhaps, whatever your situation: a time of lethargy and crushing boredom, when people find it hard to drum up energy for anything. At weekends in August there is always a mass exodus out from the city to anywhere but bricked-up places and streets of desperation; but there are always those left behind: lonely, old people with ever-ticking minds, if ailing bodies, the terminally ill, and those who simply do not know what to do with themselves. By August too much sun has sunk into our brains, the pavements look tired, people are drooping, flopping and gasping for water; then London needs thunderstorms and downpours, then the angst of inner city life is driven out of our ever-calculating brains, and we can listen to the promenade concert with a sense of quiet, if solitary enjoyment and pray for the arrival of September. Debussy knew this mood of inertia well: you hear it in his orchestral piece called 'Nuages'.

ANOTHER DAY IN WALWORTH: East Street, Liverpool Grove

On another day, we might penetrate further into Walworth by going down East Street, laid out in 1952 and celebrated for its market and the birth place of Charlie Chaplin. At the Old Kent Road end, we might note on the right hand side as we go down the new doctors' surgery and health centre: 1990's space age architecture; turning down into Elstead Street, on the left the Huntsman and Hounds pub, 1892, grandiose and confident, and opposite the Pembroke College Mission and its church St Christopher's, the hall built in 1892, the church above in 1908. All around here there is a wide variety of housing over a one hundred year period. Crossing Flint Street we glimpse the four gabled street front of the old school built 1875, now the English Martyrs RC Primary School, with the English Martyrs Church, 1902, architect: F.W. Tasker, close by in Rodney Road. You can buy all types of produce in the market: tennis balls and plastic recorders, peanuts, bounty bars, four for £1, football T-shirts. Everyone is too preoccupied bargain searching for interesting architecture, but the Masons' Arms is a grandiose pub from the end of the last century, three-storeyed, with much decoration, and seems calculated to bring in more custom than the Baptist church, built in 1896, across the road, with a mean looking little turret.

At the Walworth Road end we turn left, and are soon into the Liverpool Grove Conservation Area. Buildings of different periods, and contrasting styles can be studied around here: the flamboyant Edwardian shopping terrace, 1906-08, the disused Sutherland Chapel, built 1842 (closed in 1904), with its austere, dour columns, the housing block opposite built in 1927 by the Ecclesiastical Commissioners of England (E.C.E.), and at the centre of the area St Peter's, built 1823-25, architect: John Soane (architect of the Dulwich Gallery). Pigeons seem at home here, more than people, squatting on the entablature; set back in its own grounds, the church tower is a startling apparition amidst the shops and clamour of Walworth Road: it rises above the four ionic columns with an almost phallic insistence. There are several other Soane churches in London: St John's, Bethnal Green, and Holy Trinity, Marylebone Road. Behind the church, to our surprise perhaps, we discover a large estate of two and three-storeyed terraces built by the Ecclesiastical Commissioners 1903-09 with the

Above: *New synagogue of the Jews in Walworth Road*, from the Illustrated London News, May 4, 1867. Located in Walw...

support of Octavia Hill, who Southwark also associates with Redross and Whitecross Cottages to the north of the borough. Merrow Street, built 1906, is one long continuous, unbroken development and there are also courtyard blocks: Saltwood Grove and Burton Grove, with other streets such as Portland Street, Wooler Street, Villa Street and Aylesbury Road branching off. There are also nineteenth century terraces: Peacock Terrace in Liverpool Grove, for example. These are people's homes, people may well be scrutinising us behind drawn curtains as we wander around here; and realising we really have no business nosing around here we would be better off picking up a bus heading towards Elephant & Castle, sit on top, and imagine the road with long garden plots instead of all the shops in front.

Opposite and below: Illustrations of Walworth Road businesses from nineteenth century trade publicity. Courtesy: Southwark Local Studies Library. R.C. Hawkey & Co had its manufactory in Old Ford, East London.
The Capital and Clothing Association advertised itself as 'the largest firm of manufacturing clothiers in the world'.

THE GIRAFFE

Above: *Surrey Zoological Gardens: the new orchestra*,
Illustrated London News, May 13, 1848. The gardens were att
to Walworth Manor House (at junction of Manor Place and P
Place). Edward Cross had his zoo here from 1831-1855, and f
shows, exhibitions, fireworks and dramatised 'representations'
staged. The music hall was built in 1856, and finally demolish
1872; the Surrey Gardens site was sold for redevelopment in 187
The Illustrated London News published other interesting engra
of the subject: 'Siege of Gibraltar' spectacle, July 3, 1847; aerial
of the gardens, showing music hall exterior, and interior vie
music hall, July 19, 1856; dinner to the guards, August 30,
Other prints include a view of the Elephant House; and of the
with other structures in the background, (lithograph by F. A
1840's).

Opposite: The gardens are commemorated today by this p
Penton Place; also by the Surrey Gardens Arms in Chapter Road
the Surrey Gardens Memorial Hall in Penrose Road (Sunday S
of the Metropolitan Tabernacle). They are vividly recreated in t
David Bratby's murals in the Elephant & Castle subway.

Opposite: *Men's club and tavern of the Robert Browning Settlement*; from Southwark Annual, 1902. Courtesy: Southwark Local Studies Library. The settlement was founded in 1895 and based at the York Street Chapel (see illustration in Leisure Hour, 1895). Its first warden Rev. Herbert Stead is famous for his campaigning work for state pension legislation, commemorated on a plaque on the above building, sold to the London Labour Party in 1958, and now known as Herbert Morrison House. The HQ of the settlement today are at Fellowship House, 3 Browning Street, part of the settlement since 1911.

Above: *Walworth Common Schools, Westmoreland Road*; architects: Henry Jarvis & Son; from the Builder, January 9, 1875. Westmoreland Road lies at the southern end of Walworth Road; the schools were situated close to St Stephen's Church, and infirmary and workhouse, now all gone.

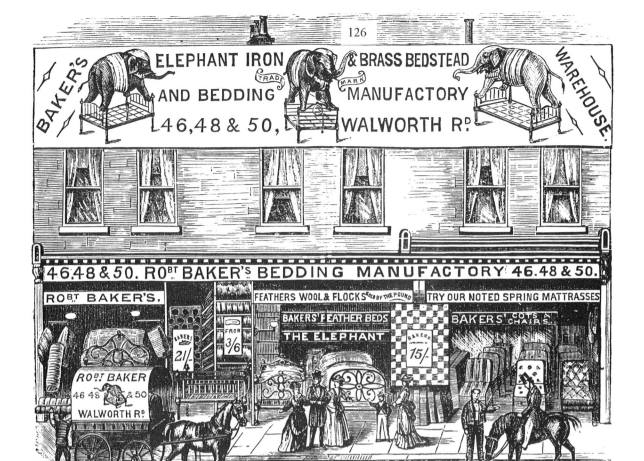

Above: The ubiquitous elephant makes another appearance. The uppermost end of Walworth Road vanished with the redevelopment. Courtesy: Southwark Local Studies Library.

Opposite: *H. & A. Holland's* were pastrycooks, fancy bread and biscuit bakers; also agents for Horniman's pure teas; they had four other shops, including one at 98 Blackman Street (lower end of Borough High Street), and one at 384 Old Kent Road. Courtesy: Southwark Local Studies Library.

Opposite: *Hay Sangster & Co*, at Cumberland Place, Newington Butts, were dealers in: 'barley, oats, tares, whole and patent groats, German paste, finest Scottish oatmeal, German yeast, flour, Scotch and Pearl barley, Indian corn, bird seed, etc, etc'. Courtesy: Southwark Local Studies Library.

Opposite: Water-colour, c. 1969 by Norman Janes showing *Newington Butts* (shops on left now demolished), leading into Kenington Park Road, with the tower of old St Mary's in the background, built 1876, architect: James Fowler; the modern church, built 1957-58, architect: A. Llewelyn-Smith lies behind. The buildings to the right, at the top of Kennington Lane still stand. Courtesy: South London Gallery.

Below: *Alldridge Brothers, general furnishing ironmongers*, had their premises at 203 and 205 Newington Butts, on the corner of Newington Crescent. The firm was taken over by Pullin Bros in the 1880's who advertised further services of locksmiths, gas-fitters, bell-hangers, and plumbers. Courtesy: Southwark Local Studies Library.

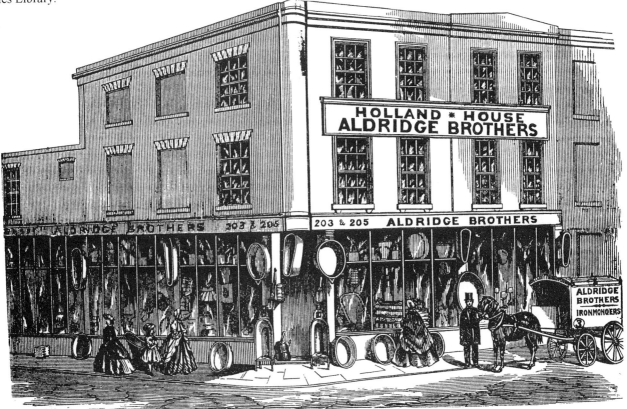

A PARK FOR THE MILLENNIUM

Close to the centre of Southwark something unusual is happening: the creation of a new community park to be completed at the turn of the century. In 1965 there were 39 acres, today there are 135 acres of open space: open space which became known as Burgess Park in 1973, after Councillor Jessie Burgess, Camberwell's first woman mayor. The informative Burgess Park Bulletin of Summer 1996 introduces us to Groundwork Southwark (a branch of the nationwide Groundwork Trust working for environmental improvement, and the involvement of local people), which is master-minding the project. Their leaflet fills us in on chronology from 1832 when the area was marshland and farmland, to a hundred years on when it was an area of dense housing and factories, followed by clearance of bomb-damaged sites in the 1950's. Three aerial photographs at Chumleigh Gardens show us the changing landscape in 1962, 1975 and 1992. Another chronology informs us of Burgess Park Committee meetings which started up in October 1995 and which are open to representatives of the widest possible range of local organisations. Fifty years on after its first proposal we learn, perhaps to our dismay: 'there is no master plan, and no money to build it'. And so, behind closed doors much frantic activity is afoot: reports, surveys, papers and documents, leaflets and brochures pour forth as all possible funding sources (to raise the estimated cost of about £30 million) are targeted from the lottery monies to local businesses. The past is researched and dug up, and a booklet written by Tim Charlesworth is in the pipeline.

Here is a fantastic opportunity to create a new vision of community: a place where the real needs of human beings can be expressed; a place dedicated to the refreshment of mind, body and soul, which demonstrates the complex inter-relatedness of all sections of the community.

I was there one hot Sunday in August. I was there for a local history tour; we were a strange septet of assorted people, who wandered around with a recently appointed Parks Ranger Services assistant; sometimes we strayed apart, broke up into two's and one's, often seemed to disagree ... I looked at all the people in the park: there were more of them than us: they were here for physical delights: frisbee throwing, perspiring games of football, jogging, fishing and sunbathing.

What struck me most, as often elsewhere, was how grass and natural wasteland quickly reappears once the built environment goes; but beneath the ground are the remains of streets, the old canal, drains, cables and other services. Again, we are struck by the relentless march of time, by the endless building, demolition and rebuilding which we encounter wherever we stray in the capital city. Indeed, it is perhaps miraculous that anything from the past at all manages to survive in the onward assault towards the Millennium.

St George's Church in Wells Way, built 1822-24, closed in 1970, the church moving to the Trinity Centre nearby; it became vandalised and was gutted by fire, but saved from demolition by the Southwark Environment Trust, and has now been converted into private flats. Crossing over Wells Way and walking down the pathway covering the site of the Surrey Canal we encounter the stranded lime kiln from the works of E.R. Burtt & Son, clearly visible in the drawing used on their letter heading. Other big works, all gone now, included R. White's lemonade factory in Albany Road, and Watkins Bible Factory in Cowan Street (South London Art Gallery has a drawing of the factory from about 1870). If we penetrate Newent Close, off Coleman Road, we will discover, to our considerable surprise perhaps, early nineteenth century stuccoed villas mixed in with Gloucester Grove Estate (built 1971-77, with 1,210 dwellings). To the west, off Camberwell Road, it is a pleasure to stroll around or sit in Addington Square, with its early nineteenth century houses and terraces, reminding us of the area's more affluent days.

Returning to the park, and moving forward in time to the very beginning of our own century, we find a gift from Mr J. Passmore Edwards, responsible for financing so many public buildings: the old library and baths (with two separate entrances); although stranded today, the buildings have an eccentric, Edwardian charm, and are thankfully occupied, currently by Groundwork Southwark, and the long-established Lynn Amateur Boxing Club.

If we are growing weary of all this brickwork, of human effort and strain, then a delightful oasis is at hand. If we are lucky to be here on an afternoon, Tuesday, Thursday or Sunday, we will be able to penetrate the old almshouse buildings of 1821, the former Friendly Female Asylum for Aged Person who have seen better days. The Council's Park Ranger Service is now based here. The department is very community orientated, organises many events, and produces many attractive leaflets. The building also provides conference, exhibition and workshop space and a café has recently opened; but we have come here to find solace in the gardens, largely unsuspected from the outside, come to visit Chumleigh Gardens: the English garden lies in front, and behind the Mediterranean, Islamic, African and Oriental gardens; all this is an initiative of students from the European Community heritage campuses held at Burgess Park in 1992 and 1993. A colourful leaflet introduces us to the ethnic characteristics, and some labelling enables identification. Strolling in these beautiful gardens,

Above: *The Islamic garden at Chumleigh Gardens*; a drawing by Lynda Durrant.

Above: *The front of Chumleigh Gardens*; the English garden, and the old almshouses; a drawing by Lynda Durrant. The old almshouses belonged to the Friendly Female Asylum for Aged Persons who have seen better days; the central wing dates from 1821, the two side wings from 1844 and 1847. The tower of St George's, Wells Way, is in the background. Both drawings are courtesy: Parks Ranger Service, Southwark Council.

Opposite: A drawing from the letter heading of *E.R. Burtt & Sons*, est. in 1816, Portland cement and lime burners, based formerly at 32-35 Canal Bank; also wharfingers, barge owners and haulage contractors. Courtesy: Southwark Local Studies Library. The lime kiln has been preserved in the western part of the park. South London Gallery has two water-colours by Guy Miller showing the lime kiln and farmhouse in Burtt's Yard.

LIME WORKS, SURREY CANAL CAMBERWELL SE

we are removed to another dimension, far from the struggles of inner city life, far from the uncertainties of life at the turn of the century. All around the back wall are Camberwell beauty butterflies: incorporated into the wrought iron railing, they are more elegant than those in Old Kent Road and their presence here seems entirely right.

At night-time the place goes very quiet: you can walk around here and see absolutely no one. The old houses in Cobourg Road hold many secrets, contain memories of many people long departed. The blocks of Gloucester Grove are lit up and with their staircase drums could be a blackcloth for some urban operatic fantasia. Here you can sense time past, present and future converging and spinning away into the heavens; the fountain in the boating lake, created in 1982, goes on spurting its jets, but night-time here is for the waterfowl and swans and for individuals seeking solace in wide open spaces, and for the park to be finally left alone to brood on all it knows or will ever know.

BOROUGH OF CAMBERWELL · PUBLIC LIBRARY (PASSMORE EDWARDS) PUBLIC BATHS AND WASHHOUSES. WELLS ST S.E.

Above: An illustration from the London Argus, July 19, 1901. Maurice Adams is also the architect of the South London Gallery/Camberwell Art School complex. The above buildings still stand, somewhat stranded, situated on the corner of Burgess Park, on land formerly belonging to Lord Llangattock. The facade of the library, with the tall chimney behind looks impressive when seen from Albany Road. The 1912 Camberwell Beauty mosaic on the southern wall comes from the works of Samuel Jones Ltd, gummed paper firm (formerly in Peckham Grove).

The Coronet Theatre stood formerly in Wells Street (now Wells Way), and South London Gallery has an oil painting, 1951, by Christopher Lawrence, and a chalk/water-colour drawing by Dorothy Blackham of this subject.

Above: A lithograph by C. Burton, printed by P. Simonau of *St George's Church, with the Surrey Canal in the foreground.* Other contemporary prints of the subject include: an engraving by Schnebbelie for the Gentleman's Magazine, 1827, and a coloured lithograph (with carriages and departing congregation) by J. Goddard, 1827. The church's architect, Francis Bedford also designed Holy Trinity, Trinity Church Square, and St John's, Waterloo Road. The First World War memorial of Christ on a plinth was erected in 1920.

There is an account of the church 1824-1974 written by Joan Edmonds, and its work as a mission church within the Trinity College Mission is covered by *Trinity in Camberwell: a history of the Trinity College Mission in Camberwell 1885-1985*, by Lawrence Goldman.

The most striking artistic evocations of the canal must be by Algernon Newton (1880-1968) whose silent, haunted, dream-like London canal and street scapes are most memorable. His oil painting 'House by Surrey Canal, Camberwell', 1935, is held by the Tate Gallery. (Exhibition catalogue published by Sheffield City Art Galleries, 1980).

South London Gallery has views by: Norman J. Barker, Dorothy Blackham, Eric Doitch, Norman Janes, Russell Reeve, Jacques Warren, and W. Whatley.

The Grand Surrey Canal was built in 1801-10, and closed in 1971, and was filled in; it ran from Surrey Commercial Docks to near Camberwell Road; a branch to Peckham was added in 1825-26. The bridge just north of the Gloucester Grove is a bizarre survival, recently renovated.

DAVID TEBBS' FORT: Towards the discovery of a painting's subject on North Peckham Estate

The search for David Tebbs' 'Fort' took me, one early June afternoon, into a strange territory.

After letters and telephone calls, I managed to meet the artist himself in his studio in Vauxhall Street (opposite the gasometers), one weekend in May when artists there opened their doors to all and sundry. There were the plates of peanuts, the small beakers of red wine. Surrounded by his students and friends, I took out my photograph, grabbed some conversation and was promised slides and details.

I walked down through Burgess Park that hot afternoon in search of his subject of some 15 years ago; around the lake and through into Wells Way, and branching off into New Church Road. Near to the Southampton Way junction, stranded and from another era, is the six-storey block Evelina Mansions, built in 1900 by the 4% Industrial Dwellings Co Ltd. With its friezes, iron railings, and entrance arches we are reminded of the Guiness Trust buildings in Snowfields, Bermondsey. Adjacent is a business called Architectural Rescue, the yard crammed full; a notice informs us it sells original old doors, floors, fixtures and fittings. Southampton Way contains much council housing on the right, the rambling premises of the Camberwell branch of Southwark College, and several old terraces to the left; growing weary of all this, it is a pleasure to find a pretty, early nineteenth century cottage at the bottom end of Peckham Grove, its stone lions guarding the entrance, and on the pavement an old street lamp and a drinking trough donated by St Luke's Band of Mercy. There is a strong scent of bread in the air, and at Unit 17, on the Samuel Jones Industrial Estate, is the Sunsplash Bakery which has shops in Bellenden Road and Rye Lane.

The tall, yellow lift shafts of the North Peckham Estate are now in view: we are close to our location, and through the fencing erected by Laing Homes on their construction site, we glimpse the adventure playground depicted by David Tebbs some 15 years ago. The mural has gone, the hut-like building is different, the playground has shut down, and the site looks threatened. The adventure playground in Bethwin Road, on the other side of Walworth Road is in a similar desperate state: the 1979 on the concrete fencing depicting historical scenes has deteriorated, and within the playground one will find the forgotten 1980 group portrait with African masks, painted by Jane Gifford and helpers.

We pass W. Uden & Son, funeral directors on the corner, and go down into Commercial Way, and then the side turning Pentridge Road to the left to approach our subject more closely. On one side of the playground is the Bradfield Youth Club which offers 'the art of kicking and punching', on the other side the 1953 St Luke's Church, replacing the 1877 building: red-bricked, asymmetrical, flat-roofed and with windows of varying sizes, it looks as stranded as the 1870 Baptist church to the north. A little black girl comes home from school, goes down the slide on the mound beside the church, goes to and fro on a swing and then has gone.

This estate, designed in 1965 and completed in 1972 containing 1,433 dwellings, is home for hundreds of people you and I will never know; yet part of the estate in Commercial Way has been ripped down: reduced to hideous piles of stone and rubble. On walls around the estate a poster from 1966 still survives: an open forum on 'Does God really exist?' was staged, it appears from 15th-19th April, 1966 in the North Peckham Tenants Hall. On one poster someone has scribbled 'Yes', and someone else 'Not on North Peckham' in reply to that rhetorical question.

The moods of this place are too confused, too contradictory; it had been a hot June afternoon, and grown weary with trudging and looking, I had to get away and back to Bermondsey.

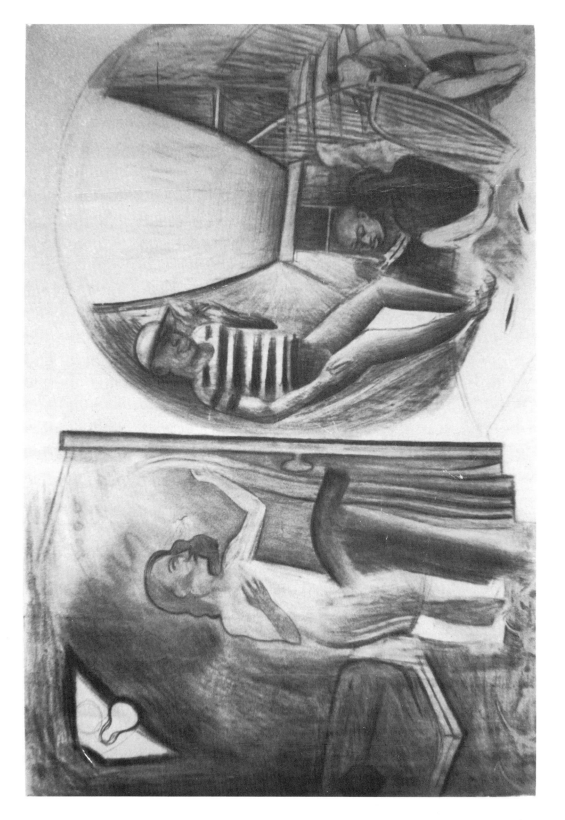

Above: *Skag kids*, charcoal drawing, 1985, by Yolanda Christian. The artist writes: ...a horrible time in my life. I lived alone on the North Peckham Estate, the design of which allowed organised crime and gangs to develop. I had my own personal gang who sat on the steps leading up to my flat and my neighbour Steve. I used to step over them as they rolled joints and 'chased the dragon' ... Around this time I suffered great anxiety at night, sleeping with a hammer next to me. Whenever I called the police it was invariably too late. Drawing the scene was an attempt to gain some sort of control. Shortly afterwards

IN AND AROUND PECKHAM ROAD AND
CAMBERWELL CHURCH STREET

Walworth Road leads into Camberwell Road and down into another locality, the centre of the former Borough of Camberwell; bus 42 (coming from Liverpool Street) will take you down there from Bermondsey passing down Albany Road, terminating at Camberwell Green. To the right is Camberwell New Road, ahead lies Denmark Hill, and to the left is Camberwell Church Street, with the dominating spire of St Giles' Church. Camberwell Church Street leads into Peckham Road with its municipal and public buildings, including the South London Art Gallery. You may feel that this is not a place to linger about in for long: this is Southwark Council Land, a place of officialdom, you may say. You will see the officials with their files and bundles of papers bounding up the steps to the 1934 Town Hall, architects: E.C. Culpin and R.S. Bowers, replacing the old 1872 Vestry Hall, and to the adjacent 1904 building, architect: E.T. Hall, across Havil Street, previously part of St Giles Hospital, and on the site of the 1827 Vestry Hall. High up, over the sundial you read the motto 'Do today's work today'. Late eighteenth century houses, now council buildings, lie adjacent: the former Camberwell House was a school known as Dr Wanostrocht's Academy and from 1846 to 1955 a private mental home; and across the road is a longer terrace, next to Lucas Gardens, named after a former Camberwell mayor. Compare and contrast the council buildings, an academic teacher may demand, and you may well conclude that by 1934 an insensitive, brutish mentality had set in: discordant tall pilasters and a ship's bow are encased in punishing red brick-work, railings have changed, sundials are out.

In the foyer of the Town Hall, you can collect council literature, beautifully designed, state-of-the-art graphic design, everything politically correct. Out goes the Southwark Sparrow newspaper, in comes Southwark Life, full colour and tourist brochure-like: the summer 1996 issues promotes with aggressive confidence new developments in the borough: a new health and leisure centre Peckham Pulse, converging cultures and schemes at Burgess Park, the annual Southwark Show, Dulwich Picture Gallery and its European roots, and the emerging network of specialist museums and historical attractions. You can pick up a booklet on Southwark's secondary schools, full of photographs of teachers and children happily engrossed in learning: be gripped by a booklet on leisure facilities, which has a cover design showing athletes out of this world and way above the clouds. *Southwark and its place in Europe* is another exciting booklet, and a folding sheet Southwark Riverside (designed and produced by Stairway Communications) uses artistic distortion for clever tourism promoting effect in a riverside panorama.

If you are interested in the visual arts, you will come to Peckham Road to visit the South London Gallery. I have come here on several occasions to visit unusual and stimulating shows: exhibitions organised by Mr Ken Sharpe, shortly before his retirement: 'The Southwark Art Collection Show' in 1988-89, and 'A slice of Southwark' in 1991 (contemporary art with a Southwark theme, or by Southwark artists). In 1996 there was a show arranged by the Tate Gallery of work inspired by the old Bankside Power Station, before it is converted into the new South Bank Tate. It must be hard to extract anything aesthetic from such a gigantic, functional place, but the large pastel works by Anthony Eyton seemed to me to be communicating the once-chaotic energy of a place now at its end. When I was there people strayed in and out, an official sat behind a tall desk, occasionally she would raise her head to see who was there. We approach the exhibition hall through a corridor decorated with busts of Ruskin, Browning and George Frederick Watts; in the big white hall itself both we the visitors and exhibits often look stranded there, I thought. It is not the done thing to talk to anyone in an English art gallery; here as elsewhere people stray in, have a look, say nothing, and stray out. What is art? Who are artists? The art world of today seems as troubled and chaotic as society in general is; we can go away from contemporary exhibitions with a pronounced sense of disturbance. It is best to quickly find something more natural, less artificial.

Close by is the beautiful churchyard of St Giles; more peaceful than Lucas Gardens, the trees here are mature, squirrels and thrushes are at home here and we will find ourselves freed of disturbance if we sit here quietly. Possibly ashes of deceased people are scattered here, quietly, sadly. At St Giles churchyard people come to say a final goodbye and start afresh. Architectural students probably come here too: old St Giles Church was rebuilt after a fire in 1841 and the new church we see today was designed by Sir George Gilbert Scott and his partner W.B. Moffatt in 1845; he was then at the start of a major career as England's most important exponent of the High Victorian Gothic style, and it is to him that we owe the Albert Memorial and St Pancras Station frontage and hotel. There is inside a brilliant eastern window, by Ward & Nixon, based on designs by John Ruskin and Edmund Oldfield, and suggesting the inspiration of Chartres. The church can be visited on Saturday mornings (9.45-12.00), and a booklet guide and history was published by Friends of St Giles Camberwell in 1987 and an account of the east window in 1992. The Bowyer family were lords of the

THE PASSMORE EDWARDS' SOUTH LONDON ART GALLERY AND TECHNICAL INSTITUTE (Lord Leighton Memorial)
Peckham Road for THE COMMISSIONERS OF PUBLIC LIBRARIES & MUSEUMS FOR CAMBERWELL. MAURICE B. ADAMS, F.R.I.B.A., ARCHT., CHISWICK, W.

Above: An illustration from the London Argus, January 8, 1898. The above does not show the adjoining Camberwell School of Arts and Crafts, which also dates from the same time and has a more dominating presence in Peckham Road. The figures on the pediment in the illustration above represent architect, painting and sculpture. A bronze nude by a former distinguished teacher at the school Karel Vogel stands at the entrance.

The gallery can trace its origins to the collection formed by William Rossiter, a teacher and author of text books. He built up a collection of Victorian paintings and the catalogue of these holdings and useful historical information on the early years is contained in a Dulwich Picture Gallery exhibition catalogue: *Art for the people: culture in the slums of late Victorian Britain*, 1994. The gallery also holds a twentieth century collection of prints, and the Southwark topographical collection.

Above: *Camberwell Vestry Hall*, architect: Edward Power; from the Builder, 1872 (includes a plan). To the left can be seen part of the former vestry hall, erected in 1827. The new vestry hall, becoming the Town Hall in 1900, was built on the site of Havil House; in its turn it was replaced by today's 1934 building.

The above illustration omits the lamps at the entrance, railings, and the three symbolic figures around the clock, and the two figures above the pilasters representing Science and Industry differ from those executed (see two photographs in CD & P in Old Photographs); nevertheless, the human activity in the foreground gives the illustration charm and interest.

manor in Camberwell for some 200 years and the church has a brass memorial to John Bowyer (died 1570) with his wife and eleven children. The manor house, demolished in 1861 stood near the site occupied today by the 17-storey block Castlemead.

The old Wilson's Grammar School, next to the church is now part of Camberwell Art College. It dates from 1882, architect: E.R. Robson; there is a little pinnacled tower to the east, and the Wilson Road side has four heraldic lions; the turrets add to the building's eccentricity. The school was founded in 1615 by a vicar of St Giles, and moved to Sutton in 1975; a history of the school was published in 1964 (second edition), its frontispiece showing a drawing of the Camberwell Church Street facade.

The two early twentieth century buildings of old St Giles Hospital in St Giles Road have a more confident air, and are more symmetrical.

To return to the architectural historians Mr Pevsner and Ms Cherry: they are in the business of telling us much that we do not know. I checked my A-Z for Sedgemoor Place off Southampton Way because here they had recorded the almshouses called The Aged Pilgrims Home, erected in 1837. A couple were just returning when I was there, and I asked if I could be let in through the locked gate. Inside, I found a beautiful garden, its existence unsuspected from the outside: a plaque in the centre records the benefactors; I was shown the stone troughs with garden flowers, the stone seats with carved legs, told that the building was renovated in the 1960's, that it was now in private ownership, a flay now occupying the former chapel over the gateway. Out at the back, I was shown slabs of slate recording the names of nineteenth century benefactors, dumped here presumably by builders. Backing the Aged Pilgrims Home in Havil Street is the Bethel Asylum, another William Peacock endowment, built in 1838 for '14 aged Christian females', and enlarged in 1842. There is a plaque in the centre and another on the wing to the right. A less striking building, the garden here is currently wild and uncultivated. The five-storeyed circular housing block on the other side of the road might arouse some curiosity too: dating from 1888 this was formerly a ward block of St Giles Hospital, and has been preserved and restored by campaigning groups. (see article 'Saint Giles Tower, ugly duckling now a Swan' by Tony Wilson in Camberwell Quarterly No 93, Autumn 1991).

Any student of London is aware of constantly drifting in and out of the nineteenth and twentieth centuries in the course of perambulating the streets. From almshouses of the 1830's, one is only a short distance away from council housing estates of the 1970's: the D'Eynsford Estate, 1971-78, architects: Clifford Culpin & Partners, is one of Southwark's first low rise housing estates of the 1970's. Houses have balconies, and pathways behind small walled back gardens. Mr Pevsner and Ms Cherry were also excited by the dining and assembly hall of Brunswick Park School in Benhill Road, built 1961-62, architects: Stirling & Cowan, but much less so by the Magistrates Court, 1965-69; perhaps they missed the beauty of the twelve horse chestnut trees ranged in the forecourt.

The topmost end of Peckham Road becomes Camberwell Church Street, and you might come here to swim, or do martial arts at the Camberwell Leisure Centre in Artichoke Lane; the baths were built in 1891, architects: Spalding & Cross, who also designed the more municipal-looking baths in East Dulwich Road. In Camberwell Church Street public buildings like the public library, police station, offices of solicitors and accountants intermingle with restaurants and pubs such as the Hermits Cave, 1902, and the Artichoke, 1883 (now renamed Brambles Bar). Camberwell Grove takes us away, as if by magic, into another dimension: a few steps into Camberwell Grove and we are enveloped in a mood of privacy, of civilised living, of Georgian terraces and semi-detached houses, the delight of estate agents and the affluent middle classes. This is the world of Dr John Coakley Lettsom (1744-1815), eminent physician whose villa built 1779-80 at Grove Hill stood in the grounds of a large estate. It was demolished in the 1890's. On the corner of Camberwell Grove, opposite a Greek restaurant is the old Mary Datchelor School (her charity was founded in 1726), with a 1926 extension in Grove Lane. A history of the school 1877-1977 was published by Hodder and Stoughton.

Retracing our steps to Camberwell Green, we should note another Camberwell landmark: the 1899 old National Westminster Bank building, architect: A. Williams. It stands on the site of a police station, and is currently being converted into a doctor's surgery. This is a curious building, with a top-heavy looking turret, more suited to a church, windows and an elaborate doorway at odds with the horizontal brick bands. Another curiosity is the former St Mary's Church, built 1873, architect: J & J Belcher, for the Catholic Apostolic Church in Camberwell New Road, and since 1977 a cathedral of the Greek Orthodox Church.

To conclude, one might wish to stray down Denmark Hill to see the hospital buildings (Mandsley Hospital and Kings College Hospital) and on into Champion Park to admire the italianate railway station, 1864-6, and the two bronze statues by G. Wade of William and Catherine Booth outside the William Booth Memorial Training College (designed 1932 by Sir Giles Gilbert Scott, architect of Bankside Power Station). She stretches out her right hand, he points up into the sky.

Above: *The Catholic Apostolic Church, Camberwell New Road*; architect: J. & J. Belcher; from the Builder, July 21, 1877. The church has been remodelled since war-time damage and today's church is a truncated version of the above design. The Greek Orthodox Church took over the building in 1963 and it has been a cathedral since 1977. See article by Tony Wilson in Quarterly Newsletter of the Camberwell Society, winter 1991.

Further down Camberwell New Road, on the corner of Councillor Street, is another interesting church: the former baptist Calvary Temple, 1891, with Italianate tower.

Above: *Freemasonry in South London: New Masonic Hall*, Camberwell; from *Pictorial World*, April 29, 1876. The building was situated in Camberwell New Road. Lambeth County Court is shown to the left. The street scene is interesting for its depiction of a variety of couples, perhaps hinting at the close-knit world of freemasonry.

Opposite: *On the Green*. The view is of Camberwell Green looking north towards Greencoat School, founded in 1706, rebuilt in 1871.

Above: *On Denmark Hill*. The church spire in the background is that of St Matthew's, built in 1848, and destroyed during World War II.

Four studies in 'looking': illustrations from an article 'Suburban London: the life of Camberwell', by H.D. Lowry and T.S.C. Crowther, published in the Windsor Magazine, July, 1895. T.S.C. Crowther is the illustrator.

Above: *Watching the Crystal Palace fireworks from Dog Kennel Hill*.

Above: *A local charity*.

Above: *Front elevation of Datchelor's School*, from The Architect, December 20, 1879. Over the entrance there is a bust of the founder Mary Datchelor, and her coat of arms with the motto 'My trust is in God alone'.

The former school building stands at the bottom of Camberwell Grove: a long hill which leads past a variety of housing including several council blocks, stuccoed villas, brick terraces, and detached houses. Beyond the school there is Grove House Tavern, and next door the Camberwell Bookshop. Grove Chapel at the top of the hill dates from 1819 and blends in well with the environment. Opposite lies Grove Crescent of the same date.

Returning from Camberwell Green

Rather than catching the bus 42 back to Bermondsey, or any bus going down Walworth Road to the Elephant & Castle, we could walk up Camberwell Road, branch off into Addington Square, go down Albany Road, and then into and through Burgess Park and so into Old Kent Road, up Dunton Road, and back into Grange Road, leading us back to Bermondsey. Southwark Pensioners Centre is at numbers 305-7 and here in a meeting room you will find a large mural depicting Southwark nature scenes, painted in 1993 by six Southwark pensioners. Cambridge House at number 131 is an important multi-purpose voluntary community organisation, originally established in 1889 as a Cambridge university settlement. You can read its historical development in a centenary booklet published in 1989. Its wide ranging concerns include adult education, legal advice, youth work, and 'advocacy' for people with learning difficulties. Crossing the road, at number 86 we will find three Coade stone medallions incorporated into the facade: these come from Dr Lettsom's house in Camberwell Grove.

Despite its length and noise of the main thoroughfare it is possible to find places of quietness nearby: Amelia Gardens, Liverpool Grove in Walworth Road for instance, and in Camberwell Road there is Addington Square, both the name of the square itself and the approach to it. Henry Addington was prime minister 1801-04, and was later created Viscount Sidmouth. The seven groups of buildings, terraces and houses, of irregular sizes give the square a sense of individuality, contrasting with the monotonous, high seriousness of the Trinity Church Square further north.

Albany Road will take us past an old board school, the William IV pub, the Burgess Park Adventure Playground, and the Burgess Park end of the Aylesbury Estate. The old school dates from 1877, with enlargement in 1904, and today houses Southwark's education psychology and welfare services. Its turret is a charming feature, a kind of reply, perhaps to the tower of St George's which is a dominating landmark around here. The adventure playground has a charming wrought iron gate with insects incorporated, and a giraffe's head protrudes from the building behind. Aylesbury Estate across the road is something altogether more monstrous: completed in 1977 this gigantic Southwark Council estate covers 64 acres, and has 2,434 dwellings. Thurlow Street has the largest block of all.

Above: An engraving, 1830's, of the *almshouses of the Aged Pilgrims Society* (established in 1807), for destitute Christian men and women of all denominations.

Above: *Addington Square* (*'The Secret'*), oil painting, 1954, by J.M. Paramor. Courtesy: South London Gallery. The scene depicted no longer exists, but we guess that the artist was less concerned with topography than with creating a certain psychological tension from motives within the landscape: the angular roof-top, iron railings, brick-work, fencing and the precipitous slide. The two girls are finding some solution to their problems, the boy with his ball has sunk into a state of perplexity. The South London Gallery holds other depictions of the square: an oil, 1952, by W.H. Innes; oil of old cottages, by R.B. Urquhart; and a water-colour of eighteenth century house by A. Hossack

IN THE LAND OF THE DEAD AND THE VANDALS:
Nunhead Cemetery and environs

It is likely that we will come to Nunhead to explore the Victorian cemetery, opened in 1840. Perhaps we have already been alerted to its existence through the excellent publications of the Friends of Nunhead Cemetery (FONC): their illustrated guide with its academic articles, the biographical research of Ron Woollacott, perhaps intrigued too by his *Historical Tour of Nunhead and Peckham Rye*, crammed full with details of local personalities of whom we had never previously heard, and enlivened by his neat and accurate drawings. Here is an organisation, established in 1981, which we feel has succeeded in putting a previously forgotten place back on the map, bringing together the considerable talents of diverse individuals: not only books, but also guided walks, an annual open day, recording, preservation and ecological work.

Turning into Nunhead Lane, off Peckham Rye, we progress down the lane until we reach Linden Grove to our right opposite Consort Road. As we slowly climb the slope, we sense the slow, trudging steps of countless mourners, of funeral corteges winding their way up the hill. Formerly called Cemetery Road, and lined with linden trees until the 1950's, this was once a place full of villas for the Nunhead rich. Today, we may well look with dismay at the hugue 1930's LCC blocks, notice the two tree stumps, and wonder whether we really want to be here at all.

As we approach the cemetery we become aware of strange sensations: as if we are nearing a place full of vibrant life, of unchecked nature, of forces at work which are intent on reducing our tiny existences to mere nothings. So, to penetrate this place, one must perhaps be intent and determined on some piece of genealogical research, or else be haunted by an overwhelming nostalgia, or perhaps be inspired simply by morbid curiosity. Reaching the entrance gates, we sense that we have arrived at an eccentric, strange kind of place; we note the upturned torches (symbolising extinguished life), the snakes biting their tails (symbolising eternal life); the two gate lodges with their mausoleum-like chimney pieces were designed by the eminent architect James Bunstone Bunning. His masterpiece the Coal Exchange in Lower Thames Street was demolished in 1962. To our right we will be struck by the gigantic pencil-like granite monument, not a tombstone, but a memorial to the five Scotsmen who agitated for parliamentary reform in the 1790's, and were punished with transportation to Australia; the Anglican pinnacled chapel by Thomas Little (in 1974 an attempt was made to burn it down) is at the top of the main avenue, with a diversity of memorials of varying shapes and types gathered around on both sides. It is as if the Victorians are trying to tell us that we are now entering another dimension of being, that we are now penetrating the very mysteries of existence.

The small party of people gathered there for the guided walk one Sunday at the end of October, as the leaves finally fell, was a strange one, I thought: one romantic figure in a tail coat, and with earrings galore had appeared from who knows where; the figures gathered there stood around the guide, immobile, unblinking, looking almost like human obelisks. I knew that no communication would be possible; and indeed after the walk, the hardy, natural historian guide quickly sped away alone in his car. As we stumbled around the pathways, angles, crosses, urns, broken columns all beckoned to us this way and that: I felt lost in the chaotic, dream world of the Victorian dead, not really sure of amongst whom I was walking. I noticed the recurring symbol of the two clasped hands – the clasped hands both of farewell and reunion – but we were also quickly made aware that this is a place for vandals and thieves. Yet once again, I was being jerked into a state of disturbance. Our guide led us to the cemetery's most ornate and extraordinary memorial: the 1865 Greek revival-style tomb of John Allan, a Yorkshire ship owner, and pointed to the mutilated urns, the angels and cameos yanked out. The Stearns family mausoleum (Mrs Stearns was apparently at rest there for only a year) is now empty. It is an unusual structure, built in 1900 by Doulton & Co with interesting Romanesque-style decoration over the doorway. Restoration we understand seems imminent. Also nearby are the tombs of Vincent Figgins, typefounder, Sir Charles Fox, engineer and builder of Crystal Palace, the inventor Bryan Dorkin, and the Nunhead monumental mason Henry Daniel. Heading north the disturbance of World War I intrudes with the two grave sites maintained by the Commonwealth War Graves Commission. To the right of the first site we stared aghast at the empty plinth where there was once a life-size bronze statue of a boy scout, commemorating the Leysdown boating disaster in 1912 involving eight Walworth scouts. It has been replaced recently with an open stone book recording their names.

As we emerge into the modern-day burial areas, close to the south entrance gate, we experience a different kind of anguish. We realise at once how mean we are to the deceased of today: we can afford only small headstones, the grass must be kept neatly mown. Regimented, cut down to size, the deceased of today are not allowed the stature the Victorians thought they deserved with elaborate memorials, nor are they permitted to dream away their eternity amidst the profusion of unchecked nature.

Opposite: *Central part of the for Camberwell Reception Centre in Gordon R now a home for unmarried mothers.* Woollacott made an acrylic painting of subject in 1979, showing the single-storey f office, now gone. South London Gallery water-colour drawings of exterior and interic Guy Miller. A design for the complex published in the Builder, 1878.

Opposite: *Central part of the almshouses ow formerly by the Metropolitan Beer and W Trade Society;* the forest of chimney stacks g the building a quaint charm; the gothic s contrasts with the Tudor style of Beesto almshouses nearby in Consort Road.

Opposite: *Mural on the side wall of the Linden Grove Community Centre;* the new railings have not deterred the paranoid vandal who has just made his own contribution.

Only by straying away from guided walks, by being alone with ourselves, does it become possible, perhaps to surrender ourselves to the true mood of the Victorian cemetery. I believe we can then hear the eloquent, yet troubled voice of Edward Elgar's cello rising up from its very midst: celebrating and lamenting the relentless rise and fall of all individual lives, of the birth and blossoming and decline of human enterprises, of the vastness of time past, present and future. We can hear both lachrymose lamentation, and soaring ecstasy as we wander in this chaotic, dream world of the Victorian dead. Other moods take over: the voices of all these souls seem to be urging us onwards, seem to say: depart, go, go back into the world of the living and do what you must, we are behind you, we are your ancestral voices, we are the music makers and the dreamers of dreams.

And so we must climb down from these heights, return to central Nunhead, and to our everyday selves and preoccupations and seek out buildings of interest and character and an unusual piece of mural art. Back in Nunhead Lane on the corner is the Linden Grove Community Centre. On a wall facing Nunhead Green we will find an interesting mural made by an American artist Helene Halstuch with help from local young people in about 1982. Sadly, to protect it from further vandalisations, it has been recently fenced in with iron railings. In the foreground are three youths, staring at us questioningly: two black, one white. They do not heed the scene depicted behind them: a Victorian family in very different attire on its way to the cemetery, and a Tilling coach and horses. The exploding fireworks remind us that Charles Thomas Brock had his firework factory in the field nearby until 1875 when he moved to Norwood.

The Pyrotechnists Arms across the road at Nunhead Green, dating from the 1860's is another reminder, and the pub at the other end of the green, the Old Nun's Head Tavern, rebuilt in 1934 reminds us of the place name's origin, with its possibly sinister background. Next to the tavern is an antiques business Peter Allen Antiques Ltd, and on the other side of Gordon Road a 1950's Salvation Army building. It is always agreeable to discover almshouse buildings, and here at Nunhead Green we will be delighted to find the almshouses erected by the Metropolitan Beer and Wine Trade Society in 1853, designed by William Webbe, and owned since the early 1970's by Southwark Council. They were in danger of being demolished but the Nunhead Residents Association managed to prevent this, but not the row of almshouses Albion Terrace, built in 1872, adjacent in Gordon Road, which made way for the 1978 Peckham Society award-winning housing development Barton Close.

Consort Road and Gordon Road lead us northwards away from the green towards Peckham High Street, and we will find other interesting philanthropic buildings in both roads. On the corner of Consort Road is a single storey, old relief station (providing food and clothing), opening in 1901, now some 95 years later it has quaint charm and is now used as a clinic. Just a little further ahead on the opposite side of the road we can delight in another set of almshouses: Beeston's almshouses (Gothic style) built in 1834 by the Worshipful Company of Girdlers and named after a sixteenth century master there, Cuthbert Beeston. His almshouses were founded near London Bridge in 1582, and moved to Nunhead when the site was needed for the building of the new bridge. The 1960's single-storey wings blend in well with the Tudor style terrace in the centre of the grounds. As I went out, I met the warden coming in. 'Have you found who you wanted?' she demanded, so I had to explain my purpose. After all, almshouses are private places, we can admire them from the street, but have no business nosing about.

In Gordon Road we discover an intimate library building at one end, and an imposing workhouse edifice at the other. The library exudes charm and warmth; it was built a century ago in 1896, one of the many library building benefactions of Passmore Edwards. The date is inscribed just below the gable, and the two roof-top scrolls are elegant details. But they could not protect this building from vandals; oh yes, the vandals again. Mr Woollacott informs me that in the early 1980's the brass art nouveau door handles and entrance lamps were yanked off and carted away to where no one knows. Dare one suggest that a society that often tries hard to deprive its members the opportunity to make any kind of decent living, which creates so many obstacles and frustrations, which offers only criticism and silence rather than encouragement and approval will engender destructiveness and criminality? Think of the violent energy these perpetrators must have possessed.

Passing on up Gordon Road, where most of the houses date from the 1870's, we will come eventually to the old Camberwell Parish Workhouse, later Camberwell Reception Centre, known locally as the Spike (a reference presumably to the railings on the two side walkways), or the Big House. The chapel at the rear and the reception office in front have been demolished and the rest of the buildings converted into flats. The main building of 1878 facing the road has a gigantic presence today and seems well fitted for its task of inspiring fear and dread. We are now close to Peckham High Street; feeling giddy with so much time, almost deranged by a sense of disturbance, it is best to return home quickly, eat a meal, play some Beethoven to revive our survival sense, and try to get some sleep.

Above: *Nunhead Station*; wood engraving by Rachel Reckitt, from *London South of the river* by Sam Price Myers, 1949. A dog strains after a motorcyclist; a bus struggles up the hill; Nelson appears on the boardings; telegraph wires hum with vibration; yet, despite all this manic energy there is always the opportunity to escape from the city quickly by train which will take us back just as quickly.

PECKHAM PIECE: Around Peckham High Street and Rye Lane

How do I start this piece? I had been searching all day long for some striking introductory words to capture this place, a place for many a Londoner way beyond the pale. Well, practically, the bus number 78 will take you there from Bermondsey, and I went there one afternoon to see how things had changed in the High Street since Ron Woollacott made his drawings some 20 years ago in 1977. As is so often the case, the pubs have survived: the Greyhound has attractive carvings and wrought iron, the Crown, nearby, is now renamed Sally O'Briens, and it no longer has its distinctive lamps; across the road is the Bun House, the gable bearing the date 1898, and further down the road the Red Bull with its attractive sign. Across the road from the Greyhound, Giggles is now the African Video Centre and Timograce Variety Stores, Janda is now Stuart Jago, florist, Alfred Marks is now Carousel Amusement Centre, and Mindels (leather goods) is now Stilletto expresso shoe repairs. Here as anywhere in London, High Street premises are constantly changing hands; changing so frequently that even locals easily forget what was once there. Leafing through a collection of old photographs *Looking back: photographs of Camberwell and Peckham 1860-1918* (from the Peckham Publishing Project) we may be startled to find the Bun House in its nineteenth century guise as Ye Olde Bun House, selling chops and steaks, tea and wine, sandwiches and wedding cakes.

The centrepiece of this northern end of Peckham must be the old Jones and Higgins building; at first we might mistake it for an Edwardian town hall, or civic department, but it is part of a former departmental store founded by Edwin Jones and George Randall Higgins in 1867. They opened their first shop at number 3 Rye Lane in 1867 and another shop at number 23 in 1891, and by the early twentieth century had erected the building we see today; the imposing tower with cupola was rebuilt after World War II, and is characteristically much more austere. Holdron's, established around 1882, was another big departmental store, with an arcade, and their upper storey facade dated 1894 at number 137 Rye Lane still survives above the present-day Agora Market, as well as their premises in Bournemouth Road. Carter's, the famous hosiers and hatters (main premises at 211-17 Old Kent Road, now demolished) had a branch at numbers 90-92 Rye Lane in much smaller, but equally attractive premises. Opposite Bournemouth Road is the truncated tower of another Rye Lane landmark: the Tower Cinema, which was open from 1914 until 1956.

Jones and Higgins were bought up by Great Universal Stores in 1954 and the business closed in 1980. In 1988 a modern-day equivalent opened: the Aylesham shopping centre, designed by the Seymour-Harris Partnership and owned by Capital and Regional Properties; the name refers to the Kent mining village, and the link between this place and the London Borough of Southwark during the 1984-85 miners' strike. Its brown brickwork, blue roofing, and banners and glasshouse roofing bring a sense of renewed, noisy energy to Peckham, even if the blue balconies and circular windows are fake and non-functional (symbolising our present-day gagged and vacant condition, perhaps?). In the central area of the arcade you will notice decorative floor tiling depicting birds, both realistic and abstract, the work of Steve Bunn, created several years ago to replace a brick 'planter'. There is a large Safeway Store here, as well as Dixons, Blockbuster Videos, D and A Fashions, the Wing-Tai restaurant and Leather House.

In Peckham as elsewhere in Southwark, or anywhere in London, or any other big city, one can slip in and out with ease of the nineteenth and twentieth centuries – a kind of game we can play with ourselves at this moment in time at the end of our century. If the Aylesham Centre is not quite to our taste, then we can go next to the railway station. Peckham Rye railway station, built in 1866, is sandwiched between Holly Grove and Blenheim Road; it has three storeys, is ornate and fills us with nostalgia for a more civilised age. To its right, in Holly Grove, there is a cast ironwork firm Southwell Stockwell Ltd, established in 1884. Holly Grove has had its long shrubbery for over one hundred years and this street, Elm Grove, and Highshore Road all have many attractive residences from the first half of the nineteenth century, often with semi-wild gardens which seem to transport us, as if by magic, into a more rural past, which was once Peckham's. In Highshore Road one will also find an old Quaker meeting house, now part of the Post Office building, built in 1826, and enlarged in 1843, and in Choumert Road (named after landowner George Choumert) one finds Girdlers Cottages (formerly Palyn's Almshouses), built in the mid-nineteenth century, but founded in 1609 in Bath Street in the City by the Girdlers Company. Choumert Road old board school dates from 1893.

Back in Rye Lane, full of food shops doing trade with local people, we will notice the 1890's decorative Midland Bank, with its turreted pinnacles, ground-level pilasters, and window decoration, the chunky Baptist church built in 1863, and opposite Woolworth's, the Hope pub. What hope? you may well ask; turning to John Beasley's origins book, we realise that this is all about Pandora's box; she has opened it up, unleashed all the ills of the world, and all that is left within is hope which she stares at. Perhaps Peckham people come here after

Above: *A row of shops, as in 1977, in Peckham High Street, opposite the Peckham Hill Street turning*; a drawing by R Woollacott, 1977.

Above: *The Britannia public house, Peckham High Street* (close to Melon Road), 1977; now demolished; a drawing by Ron Woollacott, 1977.

The Adam and Eve pub stood opposite – depicted by R.F. Moore, 1952 in a water-colour held by South London Gallery. Other Peckham High Street scenes held by South London Gallery: Eighteenth century houses, 1950's, drawing by Dorothy Blackham; Frank's, 1958, water-colour by W.K. Forrester; Peckham Unionist Club, 1952, by W.K. Forrester; Winchester House, 1950's, water-colour, by A.R. Laird; Winchester House, 1952, by R.H. Moore.

visiting their solicitors. Hepburns and Ralph Haeems have offices in Blenheim Grove, on either side of All Saints Church, built in 1879. You might spot the Peckham solicitors in streets around here: brainy-headed, focused on their cases, weighing things up, they must study their black clients with amusement and concern; countless noisy, demonstrative sessions must take place within their offices; they wonder how they can possibly explain that in England everything is the result of centuries of tradition, and slow, gradual evolution.

Back in Peckham High Street, one might not realise that the bingo hall stands on the site of an important Peckham building now gone: the Crown Theatre, designed by Ernest Runtz and opened in 1898. One might be tempted up Meeting House Lane, past the fortress-like Police Station, built 1893, replacing an earlier building on the same site, and the Nell Gwynn Primary School, 1935, to have a look at St John's Church, site previously occupied by St Jude's church, built in 1879. The architectural scholars Mr Pevsner and Ms Cherry have sent us scurrying up here to see 'one of the most interesting of the borough's post-war churches'; built 1965-66, architect: David Bush; one is struck by the aggression and starkness of this construction: a hugue sloping roof, and four strange towers, with an external bell, and splintered stained glass. It won a Civic Trust award in 1967. More homely places are at hand: the Beehive Pub is on the corner of Goldsmiths Road, and at the uppermost end, we can branch off with delight into Montpelier Road to enjoy the Victorian terrace on the right, with its steep gables, ornamented doorways and windows, and variegated ice-cream colours. We might feel ourselves transported here away from Peckham to some seaside resort. At the Queens Road junction there is the Montpelier Pub, of about 1853.

Back into the main highway, Peckham High Street turns into Queens Road and leads down to New Cross and the London Borough of Lewisham. In the turning Woods Road we find the present-day Peckham Methodist Church, built 1972-74, inconspicuous in comparison with the earlier 1864 building with its dominating spire in Queen's Road. Number 2 Woods Road, former premises of Carty & Son (makers of vats and wooden tanks) dating from the late seventeenth century, is possibly Peckham's oldest building. The church is dwarfed by Woods Road School, now John Donne School, with interesting facade featuring a wavy gable, pilasters and two tiny top storey balconies. From Cossall Park estate, built 1977-81 one can glimpse the old Camberwell workhouse in Gordon Road. What did the Victorian school children make of this, one wonders? There are other old houses at number 2-4 Queens Road. It is worth perambulating Queens Road as far as St Mary's Road. Numbers 142-148 are early nineteenth century, two buildings at an angle to the road and occupied by the adjacent packing removal firm Evan Cook; numbers 152-158, and numbers 2-6 St Mary's Road dating from about 1845 form a small terrace and with their gables and cast iron verandas bring elegance to this locality which does not seem quite Peckham. This sense of somewhere else intensifies as we go down St Mary's Road which has an interesting mix of buildings of different styles and periods: numbers 32-34 have great charm, yet look almost dream-like beside the hugue telephone exchange next door. They demand our attention in a way the two 1930's blocks opposite do not; yet the Peckham Pioneer Health Centre was an important world-famous establishment, providing leisure and health facilities between 1935 and 1950. The wavy balconies on the St Mary's Road facade are the only decorative feature on Sir Owen William's concrete and glass construction, the future use of which is currently unknown (occupied previously by Southwark College). You can read its history in accounts by John Comerford, 1947, and Innes Pearse and Lucy Crocker, 1943. Sassoon House was built in 1932-33 and is an important early work of Maxwell Fry (famous for his Sun House, in Frognal Way, Hampstead). St Mary's Church, 1961-62, architect: Robert Potter, replacing the old 1841 building, has four hugue glazed gables and a pitched, enveloping roof. It has a dominating presence in the centre of the road, with the sober Victorian terraces behind, and conveys the aggressive confidence of the early 1960's. Returning to the High Street, there is Orchard Mission Place, founded in 1887 and for some years rather derelict, now it is run by the International Pentecostal City Mission Inc. At 110 Peckham Road between Lyndhurst Way and Grummant Road the 1899 building, formerly premises of the Amalgamated Engineering and Electrical Union, is currently for sale. The matching extension dates from 1916.

By now we are probably weary of trudging. It is past six o'clock; shop-keepers are putting down their shutters, counting the day's takings, people are straying away, weighed down with carrier bags; Rye Lane and the High Street are emptying: worrying emptiness is descending down onto Peckham ... we note the new canopy structure at Peckham Square, 1994, architects: Troughton McAslan, with lighting which changes colour according to atmospheric pressure and guess that this structure will play some part in the Millennium celebrations.

Returning home to Bermondsey from Peckham, you have a sense of crossing continents and centuries: a sense of a vast geographical and time divide as you travel away from pounding drums, and bazaars full of lush, tropical fruit; the rhythms of Peckham today are the relentless, obsessional rhythms of a people with drenching rain and burning sun in their veins, laughter and gregarious noise. Returning from Peckham to old London is to become aware of a very different world, moulded by a very different culture and climate, breeding secrecy,

Above: *'8 Tracks and tapes, Peckham High Street*; etching, 1981, by Yolanda Christian. This was a second-hand junk shop run by a Hungarian couple.

Above: *Carlos, the Paris Cafe, Peckham High Street*; drawing, 1981, by Yolanda Christian. The artist writes (in a letter to the compiler): 'this is where labourers, art students from Camberwell Art College, the old and lonely and Peckham locals would feed up on large, economical meals; the atmosphere was good. Out of all of the Italian family that ran the cafe, it was Carlos who was overtly friendly, but somehow also shy. I became fascinated by the billowing clouds of steam that surrounded him as he served tea and coffee and somehow his sensitive face cast pale shadows'.

obsequiousness, a stinging meanness, and a relentless striving after money and status. Returning from Peckham is to have a stabbing sense of identity confusion, a sense that one belongs neither here nor there.

Above: *Peckham High Street at the Peckham Hill Street junction*; the Greyhound pub stands to the left, the former Crown (now Sally O'Brien) to the right.

Above: *The Oglander pub* (17 Oglander Road), a drawing by Ron Woollacott, 1977; approached via Bellenden Road, then Maxted Road. Sir John Oglander was a diarist (1585-1655). There are other attractive pubs at street corners nearby: The Prince Albert at Bellenden Road/Chadwick Road junction, and the Wishing Well (with a real, thatched well, bucket and water), at the Bellenden Road/Choumert Road junction.

Above: *Saturday, Belfort Road*; oil painting, 1955, by J.M. Paramor. Courtesy: South London Gallery. This unusual, interesting painting combines topographic accuracy with psychological tension, and possibly contains an autobiographical element. The terrace to the left still stands, but some of the urns have gone, as well as most of the chimney pots; the terrace beyond has now gone. Three boys are shown in an absorbed, yet disturbed state; already grown apart from one another, they seem cut off from the female activity in the background. A woman standing in front of an emerging vehicle stretches her hands towards the boy in the chequered shirt (who reappears in a collapsed state in the artist's Addington Square painting). He stands beside a prickly bush in his own patch and we sense that an unbreachable barrier has arisen on this Saturday in his small world. Belfort Road is a turning of St Mary's Road, Peckham.

RETURN TO PECKHAM: PECKHAM RYE AND EPILOGUE

On a warm February afternoon, I returned to Peckham to get my bearings in Peckham Rye Park, adjoining the ancient Common. The park celebrated its centenary on 14th May 1994, trees were specially planted, a booklet history, a compilation of extracts from diverse sources was compiled and published by John Beasley; a Friends of Rye Park organisation has been established and in the January 9th 1997 issue of Southwark News a double-page feature was published, reporting current developments, whilst also expressing residents' concern with present-day vandalism. A park such as Peckham Rye Park quite rightly deserves such attention: occupying the former grounds of Homestall Farm, it is a place of great beauty and tranquillity. Indeed, as soon as we are away from Rye Lane and the shops at its southern-most end, the vast expanse of the greenness opens up before us with powerful assurance, thrusting the houses on the western and eastern sides into the wings. On that February afternoon the sun poured forth warmth, clouds banked up in profusion and one's entire being slowed down. Today's mad world of packaged goods and services, and the ever-outstretched money-grabbing hand then seemed far away.

Entering the western gate, we encounter flower beds, water gardens and a rockery; further ponds lie ahead, we will find the 'Japanese' shelter, the gift of Prince Hirohito in 1914 and the Japanese garden. Here, to the west of the southern bridge lies a touching memorial stone (a replacement in 1993 of the original one of 1967); we read: 'In memory of Alice K. Street, M.B.E., founder of the London Flower Lovers' League who devoted much of her life to encouraging the interest of London school children in flowers, window boxes and gardens'. Remembering the gallery of busts of world war leaders at the Imperial War Museum when I was there quite recently, I was touched by such recognition. Indeed, in this secluded and intimate place, the monstrous concerns of the world of the human living seem to be of no relevance whatsoever, and the friendly creatures of this realm, the grey squirrels, robins, blackbirds and pigeons all address us with a simplicity and trust of such profundity that we know to our very core that society such as we know it today is disturbed, decadent and doomed.

At the very centre of the park lies the old English garden, the rose garden, or Sexby Gardens named after Colonel J.J. Sexby, the L.C.C.'s first Chief Officer of Parks (and author of *Municipal parks, gardens and open spaces of London*, 1899); to the south lies the arboretum, and to the east the lake with its water fowl and the newly restored trickling stream. Beyond are tennis courts, play equipment areas, a shed with batman scenes, and the grotesque structures of an adventure playground. Now, yet again, the human, fabricating world is intruding.

Returning to our starting point, we might wish to see where the Peckham Rye west side road will take us. It leads past Waverley School and on up Forest Hill Road. As in Linden Grove this is a steep ascent towards a cemetery: towards Camberwell Old Cemetery which opened in 1856, a vast sea of greying tombstones, crosses and angels, as chaotic as the world of the living. On the corner of Mundania Road is Forest Hill Baptist Church, looking more like a private school, or college dining hall, and at the Honor Oak Park junction the St Francesca Gabrini Catholic Primary School. Branching off into Brenchley Gardens, I realised darkness was setting in. I was somewhat off the beaten track up here, but went past the densely wooded One Tree Hill, and reached Camberwell New Cemetery, opened in 1927. I stared in through the locked gate at the chapel designed by Sir Aston Webb, and felt that here there was no expectation of a fuller existence as at Nunhead Cemetery, but rather a sense of perplexity, an awareness of time passing, and the obscurity of life's meaning. Across the road lies the vast Beachcroft Reservoir, hidden under the Aquarius Golf Course, a pumping station to the north, in an area known as Newlands. Up here, it was as if all the unresolved questions of existence were dissolving into vast, empty space.

Kelvington Road leads past the reservoir, and into Cheltenham Road. Here I came across a shop where everything was priced at one pound. I bought two bags of crisps from a grocery store to munch on the way back to the bus stop in Peckham Hill Road. Here I studied the murals on the public library newly created by Stan Pescott, Dave Benham and friends. Earlier that afternoon, before penetrating the park, I had strayed into East Dulwich Road. Here you find the quaintly named Goose Green, dominated by St John the Evangelist church, and on a wall lying adjacent to the vicarage a further creation by Stan Pescott with school children and volunteers, can be found: headed 'Vision of angels circa 1765; its starting point is the child William Blake's vision on Peckham Rye; incorporating the local church, part of the vicarage, two children and a dog, angels in a tree, and two figures emerging from the river, flowing into the landscape from a much longer panorama of biblical settlements, and stencilled trees teeming with wildlife and isolated words in different languages, with a burning bright tiger to conclude. Around the London painting there are words spoken by an angel in the Book of Revelation.

Opposite: *Peckham Hill Street*, etching, 1929, Francis Dodd. Courtesy: South London Gall. The church shown is St Chrysostom's, built 1 and demolished in 1963. South London Gal also has a water-colour of the church, 1952, R.F. Moore. The street (formerly Lord's Lane not a hill but is named after Mrs Martha Hill v bought the Peckham Manor House and Estate 1732.

Opposite: *Peckham Rye*, water-colour drawing by Norman Jones, 1963. Courtesy: South London Gallery. The view shown is the southern most end of Rye Lane, with the old baptist church Peckham Rye Tabernacle, (built in 1891, and demolished in 1970), in Nigel Road on the left. South London Gallery also has a water-colour of the tabernacle, 1952, by W.K. Forrester.

Above: A wood engraving by Frank Medworth, 1922. Courtesy: South London Gallery. A former part of the children's play area to the east of the park.

Above: *Peckham Rye Pond*, lithograph by A.R. Laird, 1933. Courtesy London Gallery. Pond, on eastern side of the Rye is now filled in.

Waiting for the bus to take me back home, I concluded that after all this, there could be no more words from me. After so many journeys down many streets, and into many localities, into all the conflicting moods and thoughts aroused by a contemporary, historic landscape, after hunting out countless beautiful images, I concluded that the time had come at last to draw things to a quiet, final close.

Peter Marcan, Bermondsey, February 1997.

NOTES ON ARTISTS FEATURED

ANDERSON, Stanley (1884-1966). A printmaker of great distinction and originality, he served a seven year apprenticeship to his father as a commercial engraver. An open scholarship from the British Institution in 1908 brought him to London and the Royal College of Art. He taught at Goldsmith's College from 1925 to 1940. He is probably best known for his series of 31 prints of country craftsmen and rural activity executed between 1933 (when he left London for Towersey, a village near Thame in Oxfordshire) and 1953. Between 1909 and 1923 he produced some 40 London views, mainly subjects in the City and in Westminster; and fine views of continental cities mainly in the second half of the 1920's. A meticulous observation of human work and activity is always a feature of his work. Goose Fair, Albi, 1927; Hot chestnuts, 1933; The fallen star, 1929 (an out-of-work actor cutting a down and out's hair by the Seine in Paris), are three examples of unusual subjects. Apart from the Hop Exchange, there are two other Southwark prints: George Inn 1919, and Little Dorrit's Church, 1925. The Guildhall Library has both and nine other London views. The Ashmolean Museum, Oxford, has an outstanding collection of his work. Abbott & Holder, Bloomsbury print dealers, staged an exhibition of some 50 of his prints in 1995, the first exhibition of his work in London since that at Colnaghi in 1932. There is a catalogue and article on his work by Martin Hardie in Print Collector's Quarterly, 1933. There are two self-portraits, 1910 and 1933, and he was also depicted in an etching in 1931 by Francis Dodd, and also in an etching by Malcolm Osborne.

BEVAN, Oliver (b. 1941). His work is not featured in this publication, but nevertheless he is important as an artist of the urban landscape since the early 1980's when he had a studio in Smithfield. Between summer 1985 and autumn 1988 he had a studio at Peacock Yard, Pullens Estate, and 21 oil paintings based on the Elephant & Castle roundabout and subway resulted. 'High rise', showing the Drapers Estate was purchased by the Museum of London and is reproduced in their publication *London in paint*. A subway scene 'Looking back' is reproduced in the catalogue of an exhibition he devised and selected in 1989: *The subjective city: fifteen artists respond to the city*. His impressive paintings of the White City Westway flyover are featured in a 1992 solo exhibition catalogue. Another 'subjective city' exhibition in 1993 'Witnesses and dreamers' at the Museum of London featured his car paintings.

BRATBY, David. David Bratby is a major talent in the field of large scale mural painting with which he has been occupied since 1978. He was born in London in 1955 and studied at Falmouth School of Art. He also creates mosaics, and artistic gardens.

BROOMFIELD, Frances. Born in Warrington in 1951, she has exhibited since 1977 almost exclusively with the Portal Gallery in London. Her work is in private collections throughout the world. It is in a magical realist naive style and draws on a wide range of themes, often inspired by research. Most recently she has drawn inspiration from nursery rhymes. She contributed five paintings to the 1996 Portal Gallery show 'Gardens of delight', including 'Monet's waterlilies'. Her imaginative portraits and cat paintings are especially delightful. Her work has been used for greetings cards, and she has designed book jackets for commercial publishers.

CHALLENGER, Mike. Born in 1939, the artist has lived in Park Street for some 20 years, and is a Borough Market trustee. He studied at Goldsmith's College and the Slade, and has had a prolific, and still developing career as a painter, sculptor and printmaker. In 1966 he won the Sainsbury Prize for Sculpture. In the second half of the 1980's he produced some 30 drawings and paintings of the area around Borough Market. They show much awareness of the peculiar atmosphere of this location and are very successful. Some hang in the offices of Borough Market, others in the offices of a local engineering and electrical firm; several exist as postcard reproductions. His charcoal drawings of the Wheatsheaf and the Market Porter hang in the bars of the two pubs. He showed this Southwark work at a one-man show in Southwark Cathedral in 1987. A later commission in 1992-93 from Cure's College almshouses, now in West Norwood, lead to the creation of a triptych oil painting showing the Southwark riverside from London Bridge to Blackfriars Bridge. A commission from Jeddah in Saudi Arabia in 1989 lead to the creation of some 70 topographical paintings shown at the Art Vision Gallery, Jeddah in 1990. Despite this topographical work, he has been preoccupied for many years with three-dimensional, geometric, coloured constructions (designed to hang like paintings), and an exhibition of such work was staged in September 1996 at the Bedford Hill Gallery in Great Suffolk Street. His work is in many public collections in the UK and USA. He is also a talented amateur pianist, and has a keen interest in Bach, Beethoven and Bartok.

CHRISTIAN, Yolanda. Born in Liverpool in 1957, Yolanda Christian is an inquisitive and impressionable, prolific, well organised young painter and printmaker of great persuasion. She studied at Wolverhampton Polytechnic, and then at the Slade. Her career was launched with her arrival in London: a new contemporary at the ICA on four occasions, her first show was *Peckham, People and Places*, in 1981 from which the two works reproduced here are drawn. The show was held on the premises of the Peckham Action Group and resulted from her fascination with Peckham's cosmopolitan people and shops when she was living there. An interesting article/interview was published in the South London Press, May 29th, 1981 on this occasion. Several other shows drawing on South East London life followed: *Private Lives* at Swiss Cottage Library, and *People and Places* at the Woodlands Art Gallery, Blackheath and *Across the Frontiers*, Concourse Gallery in 1983. In 1985 she travelled to China to research her Portuguese/Chinese ancestry, resulting in a travelling exhibition *Taking Root* of some 50 works. She describes one of these 'I've been on a long journey' in Printmaking Today, Vol 3, No 2, 1994. Another important journey was to the Clayoquot Sound Rainforest in 1994. Her work in the 1990's (as illustrated in her current brochure) is multi-cultural, global and spiritual in its concerns. In her 'Between Two Worlds' symbolic figures mingle with trees of life and animals in a hugue painting ten feet by five. 'A span of parched earth' by contrast is a ten foot image of cracked earth. There is also a series of prints inspired by the Bosnian war. Her work is in public collections, including those of various London hospitals.

COLE, Frederick W. A stained glass artist of great distinction and achievement with work in many churches in England, Northern Ireland, the USA, South Africa, Canada and other foreign countries. He studied at Camberwell School of Art and worked for the stained glass studios of William Morris and the Wippell Studio before starting his own studio in 1961 in Fulham. He is a Fellow of the British Society of Master Glass Painters and a liveryman of the Worshipful Company of Glaziers and Painters on Glass. In 1990 he was awarded a Master of Arts degree by the University of Kent for world-wide services to the art and craft of stained glass.

COOK, Denise. Denise Cook's picture book-style murals at the Elephant and Castle subway of wildlife and scenes from Southwark's past are exciting and vibrant; they contrast well with David Bratby's more complex creations, and seem calculated to appeal to a young audience. She was born in London in 1947 and studied at Harrow and Kingston Colleges of Art.

CROWTHER, T.S.C. An illustrator, active in the 1890's and early years of the twentieth century, he contributed to publications such as the Daily Graphic, English Illustrated Magazine, the Graphic, Temple Magazine and the Windsor Magazine.

DODD, Francis. (1874-1949). Distinguished etcher of topographical views, both British and European, and of portraits (of his contemporary artists). He studied with Muirhead Bone, another major etcher of the period, at Glasgow School of Art, and in 1903 he married his sister Gertrude. His subjects are always acutely observed and expressed with immaculate technique and all his plates are very much collectors' items. South East London scenes include: an impressive drypoint, 1914 of St George the Martyr; Kennington Lane, 1914, and 1915; Greenwich, 1915 (showing part of the Trafalgar Tavern); Belvedere Road, Waterloo, 1913; Pall Mall, 1919 and Strand with sky, 1916 (St Mary le Strand) are two impressive Central London subjects. In the mid twenties he was travelling in Europe and depicting French, Spanish and Italian subjects. An essay and catalogue of his prints by Randolphe Schwabe appeared in Print Collectors' Quarterly in 1926.

DURRANT, Lynda. Lynda Durrant is a graphic design artist (Full Circle Design in Brighton). The two drawings reproduced are from a series of postcard reproductions of garden scenes and plants at Chumleigh Gardens, Burgess Park.

FLETCHER, Hanslip. (1874-1955). For many years he worked for the Sunday Times and his drawings for the paper were later collected in *Changing London*, 1925-28, and 1933. Other London books are: *London passed and passing*, 1908; and *Bombed London*, 1947. The Guildhall Library has a large collection of his work.

FRIED, David. The work of David Fried will be familiar to those who purchased the compiler's earlier collections: *An East London Album*, and *A Bermondsey & Rotherhithe Album*. The drawings in this new publication were likewise specially commissioned and reveal the artist's deepening awareness of the emotional disturbance of those on the edge of society which is intensified by the desolation of inner city life today. He continues to work as a part-time art therapist, and in his uncompromising, direct probing analysis of aspects of the human condition many would prefer to ignore, he is an important visual commentator on our troubled times.

GOLDEN, Grace. She had a long artistic association with the Bankside area and in 1951 she wrote and illustrated *Old Bankside*, published by Williams and Norgate. Her drawings, which can vary in quality, extend over many years from the 1920's. More of her drawings, together with historical notes, feature in her *Bankside broadsheets*. The Livesey Museum has a large scale oil painting of her's at the entrance depicting the Thames at London Bridge and the South London Gallery has a number of her water-colours. The Image Library at the Public Records Office holds her equally impressive oil painting of Paddington Station.

HEPHER, David. Not reproduced in this publication, but his work should be noted. He is known as the painter of tower blocks, and had his second retrospective exhibition at the Museum of London in December 1996. A book on the artist by Edward Lucie-Smith was published on this occasion by Momentum (PO Box 12752, London E8 3UA). An earlier publication with an introduction by the artist was published by Flowers East Gallery on the occasion of his exhibition of new paintings in 1989. The tower block works, painted with meticulous realism are based on: Drapers House, Elephant & Castle ('Walworth Flats', 1977); Chiltern House, Aylesbury Estate ('Albany Flats', 1977-78); Coopers Estate, off Old Kent Road ('Arrangement in Turquoise and Cream', 1980-81), and Habington House, Elmington Estate ('Camberwell Nocturne', 1984; and 'Camberwell Flats II'). The blocks of Cotton Gardens, off Kennington Lane feature in three, more open cityscape paintings: 'The Hawk's tower', 1986-87 (depicting the abandoned industrial tower); 'Homage for L.S. Lowry', 1987; and 'Kimberly Street Flats', 1987-88. In his tower block paintings of the 1990's, graffiti is used with ambiguous effect, and paint is mixed with concrete. 'Five blocks by the Oval', 1995, depicts the Brandon Estate, as seen on the horizon.

JANES, Norman. (1892-1980). Prints by Norman Janes appear in the compiler's *Artists and the East End*, and *A Bermondsey & Rotherhithe Album*, and his output of wood engravings, etchings, aquatints and colour linocuts depicting British and foreign landscapes and townscapes constitutes an impressive and stimulating body of work. From 1945 to 196 he was Honorary Secretary of the Royal Society of Painter Etchers and Engravers. He also produced water-colours and the South London Gallery holds a small number of these. There was an exhibition of his prints in November 1996 at the Twentieth Century Gallery in Fulham. His son Michael Janes wrote an illustrated article on his life and work in the RE's Journal, No 7, 1985.

JONES, Olwen. Olwen Jones was born in London, of Welsh parents, and educated at the Harrow College of Art and the Royal Academy Schools. She is a water-colour painter and printmaker (a member of both the R.W.S. and the R.E.), and she is inspired by interiors, and gardens, and conservatory scenes in which she studies the relationship of natural forms and the more formal shapes of the man-made environment. She was featured in Michael Spender's book 'Visions of Venice', and in the magazine Create, January 1993. She has work in many UK public collections.

JUDKINS, Rod. Rod Judkins is a contemporary artist of considerable importance. He has been holding annual one-man shows at the Thumb Gallery since 1983 (later renamed the Gill George Gallery), and seems to be articulating in a unique way much of the agony of life at the end of the century: its perplexity, emptiness and alienation. His second show at the Thumb Gallery in 1984 depicted solitary, lost figures against bleak, desolate landscapes. His 1994 show had the title 'After the brittle era' (referring to the broken statues of Eastern Europe). The pressures and anxieties of men in high profile city occupations featured in his 1996 show: highly dramatic oil paintings commenting on the failure of communication, professional dilemmas and institutional paranoia. His lucid compositions make an immediate impression and he looks set to have an important career. His work is in many collections, including Worcester Museum & Art Gallery, W.H. Smith, and Goldman Sachs International.

KINDERSLEY, Richard. Richard Kindersley studied lettering and sculpture at Cambridge School of Art and in his father's studio, and in 1966 set up his own studio in London. He has had many lettering and graphic commissions from cathedrals and public buildings. He has been a consultant for the graphics and lettering on Canary Wharf.

KOSSOWSKI, Adam. Born in Poland in 1905, he studied at Kracow and Warsaw academies of art, and mural techniques in Rome. After World War II he came to London, and carried out much ceramic relief work for Roman Catholic churches throughout the UK. The Peckham Civic Centre mural was a new departure for the artist in its depiction of secular subjects. (Information from: booklet on the Civic Centre issued by London Borough of Southwark's Department of Architecture and Planning, 1966).

LAIRD, Arthur Robert. (Born 1881). Educated at Wilson Grammar School, Camberwell School of Arts and Crafts and Westminster School of Art. He was a member of the Senefelder Club and the Society of Graphic Artists; also part-founder, Honorary Treasurer and later Vice-President of the South London Group (from 1921). The South London

Gallery has several other items by him, including Winchester House, Peckham High Street, 1950's, and Salvation Army College, 1953.

LARGE, George. Born in 1936, and educated at Hornsey College of Art, George Large is an artist whose work must surely bring zest, excitement and stimulation into the lives of everyone who encounters it. A member of the Royal Institute of Painters in Water-colours since 1986 he creates vibrant, dynamic, semi-abstract compositions of stunning colour based on observation of people at work and at play. He delights in depicting his figures as powerful, muscular, physical shapes. A one-man exhibition at the Llewellyn Alexander Gallery in May 1995 was entitled 'Large's London'. His 'Cleaning St Paul's' and 'Road works, Charing Cross' were reproduced in a review article in Artists & Illustrators, August 1995. Other subjects included Waterloo Bridge, Cannon Street, Westminster Cathedral and St Katharine's Dock. An earlier one-man show at the same gallery in 1993 had a Trafalgar Square scene 'Feeding the pigeons', paintings of Maltese fishermen and women, swimmers, acrobats and jugglers, gardeners and lovers, a 'Catswoman' and a 'nautical man'. There was another one-man show in 1991 at the same gallery, and one-man shows in 1990, 1992 and 1994 were held at Duncan Campbell Fine Arts.

LAWSON, John N. John Lawson has been chief designer/artist with Goddard & Gibbs Studios Ltd in Shoreditch (est. 1868) since 1970. His designs for Christ Church in Blackfriars Road are reproduced in a booklet from the church 'Windows on the world of work'. The studios have also been responsible for two stained glass windows in St George's RC Cathedral, one commemorating the Pope's visit in 1982, the other the work of the Knights of the Holy Sepulchre (based at the church); at Express Newspapers, Blackfriars Road there are two large panels based on the five senses, and six smaller ones above the lift doors representing various subjects dealt with by newspapers.

McCORMICK, Arthur David. (1860-1943). Illustrated travel books 1894-1909, and wrote *An artist in the Himalayas*, 1893. He also contributed to periodicals such as the English Illustrated Magazine, and Illustrated London News.

MEDWORTH, Frank C. (1892-1948). He studied at the Royal College of Art; head of painting at Hull; emigrated to Australia in 1939; died in Mexico when working there for UNESCO. (Information provided by Geoff Hassell). The South London Gallery also holds his water-colour drawing, 1919, of the Dust Chute, Grand Surrey Canal; and a pencil drawing, 1912, of the art school. The Victoria and Albert Museum holds two wood engravings by him: The toilet, 1924; and Lovers, (undated).

MILLS, Dorothy. South London Gallery holds a number of her water-colours: of Elephant & Castle, 1956; the Bolton Synagogue, Wansey Street, 1960; St Mary Overy Wharf, 1969; and Surrey Docks offices, c. 1955.

MUMBERSON, Stephen. Born in 1955, and educated at Brighton Polytechnic and the Royal College of Art, he is an artist of almost archetypal manic energy and productivity. His monumental series of over 70 linocuts made between 1991 and 1994 depicts many well-known buildings and sites in central London. His pencil drawings of London subjects are equally impressive. He was elected a Fellow of the Royal Society of Painter-Printmakers in 1995; and has been a lecturer at Middlesex University since 1987. He has exhibited extensively throughout the world, and in 1992 was requested by the British Council to hold print workshops in Lusaka, Zambia, and in Harare, Zimbabwe. Art from African and other primitive and early cultures have been important influences and he has evolved a style he considers appropriate for a commentary on the society we live in today. He makes bronze ritualistic objects, mixed-media sculptures, puppets, kites and artists books, but his printmaking is the core of his work. A profile on the artist by Anne Desmet was published in the Bankside Bulletin, no 6, 1994, with a reproduction of his Lloyds of London linocut and a linocut portrait by a Zimbabwe student.

PARAMOR, J.M. It has not been possible to trace any information about this talented, atmospheric artist, but the South London Gallery holds four paintings by him from the 1950's: the two reproduced in this publication (Belfort Road, and Addington Square); Clearance area, John Ruskin Street, 1957; and Nunhead Station.

PARKER, Jen. The artist trained as an illustrator at the Chelsea School of Art. For the last 14 years she has been a full-time freelance illustrator and printmaker. Her large-scale pictorial map of the Southwark Diocese hangs in the cathedral and was executed 1986-87, based on real people; her drawing to commemorate the construction of the cathedral's new chapter house (hanging in the restaurant) is equally powerful. She has done work for guide books, especially for Bethacarr Prints and for special commemorations: a City of London drawing to celebrate 800 years of Lord Mayors, and a drawing to commemorate the 375th anniversary of the sailing of the Mayflower, for example. She was living in St George's Road in the first half of the 1980's and made many drawings and etchings of panoramic views and buildings in the northern part of the borough. Although precise and accurate, her work exudes charm and affection.

PAYNTER, Hilary. Born in 1943, Hilary Paynter is a wood engraver of great talent, commitment and social concern; not only has she been producing a distinguished body of work for thirty years based on everything and anywhere which arouses her emotions, but she has also enjoyed a successful career as a teacher, working especially with difficult children and more recently as an educational psychologist; and in addition since 1983 she has worked as Honorary Secretary of the Society of Wood Engravers, organising their annual touring exhibitions. She can be inspired by literature, landscape, political events, social tragedy, or her domestic life. Illustrated catalogues produced for her shows at Hereford Art Gallery in 1991 and Durham City Gallery in 1995 indicate her versatility. It is probably true to say that, despite the diversity of subject matter, she is teaching us at all times to understand the forces and powers which control the world: natural, political, physical and emotional, artistic and spiritual. An illustrated article on her work by Michael Blaker appeared in Print Making Today, Vol 4, No 2, 1995.

PESKETT, Stan. Born in 1939 in Epsom and educated at Epsom, Guildford and the Royal Colleges of Art, he is an artist of archetypal versatility and energy. In the early 1960's he drew inspiration from the Notting Hill Gate area. He was active in New York City from 1974 until his return to London in 1989, creating murals, sets, installations and videos. He has always been committed to public art of all kinds and to encouraging new talent and experimentation. In the 1990's he has been involved with visionary and prophetic paintings, tableaux, writing and concepts. The William Blake mural was commissioned by the Dulwich Festival in 1993. In 1996 he has been involved with sets for Peckham Varieties Theatre, and a new mural 'Time piece triptych', commissioned by Deptford City Challenge (in New Cross Road). He currently teaches at Cleveland College of Art and is working with Moorfields Primary School in Islington on a book/musical/CD Rom 'Little Boy Lost' evoking different periods of London's past.

PRINCE, Val R. Painter and illustrator active in the 1890's.

RECKITT, Rachel. (1908-96). A wood engraver, she illustrated a number of books from 1945 to 1954. Her illustrations to Sam Price Myer's *London South of the River*, 1949 are especially attractive. Her work is, however, mainly figurative, rather than topographical. A more recent book is her *Seven Psalms*, 1981. In 1990 she exhibited with three other engravers at the Duncan Campbell Gallery, South Kensington.

ROSE, David T. (1872-1964). He qualified and worked as a civil engineer, but pursued art full-time, working in water-colour and tempera, and some etching when he retired to Brighton in 1935. He exhibited at museums, local shows in Sussex, at the RA, and the Scottish RA and elsewhere. His daughter presented a collection of his water-colours to the South London Gallery in the 1960's. In addition to the two works reproduced, they hold his paintings of Borough Market and Southwark Bridge.

SCHNEBBELIE, R.B. Son of an artist of Swiss descent who worked as a draughtsman for the Society of Antiquaries, R.B. Schnebbelie was one of the artists who worked on the printseller Robert Wilkinson's project Londina Illustrata, a wide ranging series of prints of many buildings then being demolished or being altered, or changing their use. His drawings and water-colours were engraved by others. He was responsible for about a quarter of the 206 plates which were published in two volumes in 1834, in other topographical books of the time such as Hughson's *Walks Through London*, and the *Architectura Ecclesiastica Londini*. His south view of Queen Elizabeth's Free Grammar School in Tooley Street, 1813 is reproduced in the compiler's *Bermondsey & Rotherhithe Album*; and his view of St John's House, Hoxton, 1823 in the compiler's *East London Album*.

TEBBS, David. The artist has lived in South East London since 1979. He studied at Camberwell School of Art and at Goldsmith's, and currently has a studio in Vauxhall Street. He draws inspiration from his local environment, but his aim would often appear to be an escapist approach to reality rather than an involvement with it. Thus in recent work he has used the theme of an underground car park (based on that at the Camden Estate, Peckham), as a setting for figures observed at a Conservative Party conference; several parkland scenes show figures in suits almost submerged and lost in the natural vegetation, and another series of much smaller paintings depict himself sleeping. Despite this sense of disturbance, his work is lucid and technically very accomplished.

VAN NIEKERK, Sarah. Born in 1934, Sarah Van Niekerk is a wood engraver of great distinction. She studied with Gertrude Hermes at the Central School of Arts and Crafts and from 1976 to 1986 she was tutor in wood engraving at the Royal Academy Schools. She is a Fellow of the Royal Society of Painter-Printmakers , the Royal West of England Academy, the Society of Wood Engravers, and the Art Workers Guild. Her compositions are based often, but not exclusively, on countryside and rural subject matter and convey much dramatic excitement. Examples of her work are reproduced in *Engravers I* and *Engravers II* from Silent Books. Together with Simon Brett and Henry Brockway, she has illustrated the Bible for Reader's Digest; she has also worked for Dents, the Folio Society, the Gregynog Press, OUP, Rider Books and Pavilion. She is represented in many public collections.

WELLER, Anthony. (1927-91). Sculptor in fibreglass, marble and bronze; his work is to be found in permanent collections in the USA, UK, South Africa and Japan.

WHITTOCK, Nathaniel. Active 1828-51 as a draughtsman and lithographer. He published drawing books and illustrated two topographical and historical books on Oxford in 1829 and 1830.

WILKES, Jessica. Born in 1948 in Newcastle upon Tyne, and educated at Newcastle Polytechnic and Chelsea School of Art, the artist has been living and working in Southwark since 1976. She is a member of the Bermondsey Artists Group and is active in educational work in Southwark and other London boroughs. She uses traditional subject matter – the view from her studio window, fairground and circus, mythological themes, but there is also a strong personal and autobiographical element in her work. 'Prayer for my father' refers to her late father's love of cherry blossom, is also inspired by a poem of A.E. Housman and is one of a series of paintings on the theme dating back to the early 1980's, based on the local environment. The South London Gallery and the Arthur Andersen collection have versions. Sexuality would appear to be a preoccupation in her impressive oil painting 'Carousel', 1988-91 shown at the 1996 Barbican exhibition *Rubies and rebels: Jewish female identity in contemporary British art* and reproduced in the Lund Humphries accompanying book. Her statement published here is an interesting account of her preoccupations and experiences. Small paintings of trapeze artists were also shown at the Barbican exhibition. She has exhibited in a wide range of mixed shows, and had a solo show in 1996 at Eger Architects in Camberwell.

WILLIAMS, Brian. He studied at Camberwell Art School, and has been resident in Southwark for some twenty years. His portraits (oil paintings and drawings), and his prints and paintings of Southwark buildings and people, and other localities, show considerable energy and talent. He enjoys painting in East Street Market, and has made two large impressionistic paintings, and a striking drawing, based on this subject matter. He has also painted views of Borough High Street, Merrick Square, West Square and Walworth Road.

WILLIAMS, Hubert. (1905-89). The artist was a good friend of Canon Stevens and his drawings are included in the various editions of Rev. T.P. Stevens' account of Southwark Cathedral, in his booklet *Winchester Palace in Southwark*, and in 1930's issues of the Parish Paper and Diocesan Gazette of St Saviour with St Peter (Dickens' Southwark revisited series). The South London Art Gallery and Southwark Local Studies Library hold a small number of original drawings. There is a striking pictorial map of Southwark by the artist in Southwark Council's publication *Historic Southwark*, 1951.

WINKELMAN, Joseph. Born in Keokuk, Iowa in 1941, the artist pursued studies initially in English and business, before coming to England in 1968 to study at the Ruskin School of Drawing, Oxford, where he has lived ever since. He has a studio at Headington. He exhibits regularly and has work in many public collections. He is a past-president of the Royal Society of Painter-Printmakers, and an academician of the Royal West of England Academy, an Honorary Fellow of the Printmakers Council of Great Britain and a Vice-President of the Oxford Art Society. He is a printmaker of distinction and he shows great sensitivity to both the built and natural environments around him, with a particular interest in the qualities of light, time of day, and season. The two reproductions in the article by Michael Blaker in Printmaking Today, Vol 4, No 4, 1995: Tom Tower West, 1990; and Winter morning, 1990, highlight his special qualities. He has been recently commissioned to execute a set of plates of Balliol College. The journal of the RE, No 5, 1983 contains a short article by him, and he issues his own illustrated brochure.

WOOLLACOTT, Ron. Born in Lewisham in 1936, Ron Woollacott has lived in the SE15 district of London since 1942. He worked for 35 years for the Royal Mail, and now devotes himself to his life-long interests of local history research and topographical drawing. He is a founder member of the Peckham Society (its chairman from 1977 to 1982), and a founder member of the Friends of Nunhead Cemetery (its chairman since its formation in 1981). The RONC has published his two books *Nunhead Notables* and *More Nunhead Notables*. In 1995 he published his *A historical tour of Nunhead and Peckham Rye*, with his own illustrations. He has written and published numerous articles on Peckham's history since 1976 and contributed to the London Encyclopaedia. Currently he is working on the London Cemetery Company, and burial grounds in Southwark, including Camberwell Old Cemetery. His catalogue of acrylic paintings lists 59 works dating from 1974 to 1983 (with two commissions in 1986 and 1989); four water-colours date from 1982, 1988, 1990 and 1992. A wide variety of Peckham and Nunhead subjects are featured. His work is careful, accurate and a valuable record of many vanished subjects. He has exhibited at the annual shows of the South East London Art Group between 1976 and 1983.

BIBLIOGRAPHY: SOURCES FOR FURTHER READING AND PICTURE MATERIAL

I: ILLUSTRATED SURVEYS AND INVENTORIES

Copious factual information, supported by selected photographic and non-photographic material exists on all parts of the London Borough of Southwark today.

Despite the abundance of literature, it is the compiler's hope that he has succeeded in drawing together many hitherto little known, little used illustrations and has produced a text which has a strong personal, often autobiographical bias which conveys something of one individual's experiences in the borough over the period 1995-96. However, no topographical writer can ignore the weight of the past and I am especially indebted to the following authoritative sources for factual information such as names and dates of architects.

a) *The South London volume of the Penguin Buildings of England Series,* by Brigid Cherry and Nikolaus Pevsner, 1983. The Southwark section is broken down into three basic parts based on the three old boroughs: Southwark, Bermondsey and Camberwell. Within each part there are sections on public buildings, churches and then the so-called 'perambulations' which survey specific localities with references back to previous sections. There are also useful footnotes on demolished buildings. The writing is dense, and technical and normally avoids subjective judgements. The interested layman will find it useful, but hard-going and alienating in its erudition.

b) *The London Encyclopaedia,* edited by Ben Weinreb and Christopher Hibbert, Macmillan, 1983, is also highly factual, but uses many illustrations from the eighteenth and early part of the nineteenth century. It is written by a large team of local historians and local history librarians, and there are many entries for localities, streets and buildings in Southwark.

c) Another London-wide reference book with many Southwark entries is *The streets of London*: a dictionary of the names and their origins, by Sheila Fairfield, Macmillan, 1983.

d) *The Neighbourhood History Series of booklets, written mostly by Mary Boast and published by the London Borough of Southwark,* provide succinct, factual information on a wide range of subjects, extend to the present day and contain detailed bibliographies (including unpublished and non-book sources); they are based on the author's long association with the borough and her understanding (as a former librarian) of the needs and interests of most readers and library users.

The relevant titles are: *The story of Bankside,* 1985; *The story of the 'Borough',* 1982; *The story of Camberwell,* 2nd edition, 1996 (with index); and *The story of Walworth,* 2nd edition, 1993. The two new editions use a selection of photographs and engravings. Outside the series there is a booklet *Charles Dickens and Southwark,* 2nd edition, 1994.

e) *Specialist Peckham publications.* The books by John Beasley stem from the author's long association with Peckham, and his desire to enhance its 'image'; they are based on research in a very wide range of quoted sources: *Who was Who in Peckham,* Chener Books, 1985; *Origin of names in Peckham and Nunhead,* South Riding Press, 1993; *Peckham Rye Park, 1894-1994,* South Riding Press, 1994; and *Peckham and Nunhead churches,* South Riding Press, 1995 (contains some old engravings); a book on Peckham transport is due to be published in 1997. *The architecture of Peckham,* by Tim Charlesworth, published by Chener Books (a Dulwich bookshop) in 1988 is an account of mainly domestic houses, but with detailed listings of buildings of interest, arranged by period; there are nineteenth century maps and contemporary photographs.

Another important local author is Ron Woollacott who published his informative and personally illustrated booklet *A historical tour of Nunhead and Peckham Rye* in 1995.

f) *Other sources.* Many of the above authors are drawing on earlier publications. Two important publications are part of the *Survey of London* series:

Volume XXII, 1950: Bankside (parishes of St Saviour and Christchurch).

Volume XXV, 1955: Parishes of St George's the Martyr and St Mary Newington.

In addition to photographs and contemporary drawings, both surveys reproduce water-colours from the old Greater London Record Office collection, by Appleton, Buckler, the Shepherd's, Yates and others.

Camberwell is covered by two important works: *The parish of Camberwell*, by W.M. Blanch, 1875, reprinted by Stephen Marks for the Camberwell Society, containing many engravings of public buildings and personalities; an important academic study is *Victorian suburb: study of the growth of Camberwell*, by H.J. Dyos, Leicester University Press, 1961.

There are also more general, topographical accounts: *London South of the Thames*, by Walter Besant, published by A & C Black, 1912, has a substantial Southwark chapter with a wide range of illustrations; business enterprises are featured (often with illustrations) in *A descriptive account of South London, illustrated*, 1890; and *A descriptive account of Peckham and Camberwell*, 1892, written and published by W.T. Pike.

II: PHOTOGRAPHIC COMPILATIONS

The photographic holdings of Southwark Local Studies Library are exploited in three recent collections: *Southwark, Bermondsey and Rotherhithe in old photographs*, compiled by Stephen Humphrey, Alan Sutton Publishing, 1995; *Camberwell, Dulwich and Peckham* (Britain in old photographs series), also compiled by Stephen Humphrey, Alan Sutton Publishing, 1996; and *Peckham and Nunhead*, compiled by John D. Beasley (Archive Photographs Series), Chalford Publishing, 1995. The later two collections contain some duplicated material, in its turn duplicated by an earlier collection: *Looking back: photographs of Camberwell and Peckham, 1860-1918*, published by Peckham Publishing Project, 1979.

The three recently published collections have short introductions, brief captions, and also include a small amount of non-photographic material.

III: EXHIBITION CATALOGUES, SOUTHWARK IN/AND ART

Two important catalogues of local history exhibitions organised by Southwark Council are:

In the clink: catalogue of an exhibition of Southwark's local history from Roman times to the present day, 1972; and *On the road*: 2000 years of Southwark's Old Kent Road, 1974. Many kinds of picture material, and artefacts are catalogued. On the Road, for example, features photographs loaned by the Pembroke College Mission.

South London Gallery has an important topographical collection, and part of it was exhibited in 1988, with an accompanying list. In 1991 an open exhibition *A Slice of Southwark* displayed over 80 works with a Southwark theme, or by Southwark artists. The catalogue indicates the artist's place and date of birth, and date of taking up residence in Southwark.

Reproductions of paintings of Camberwell and South East London interest are included in a recent biographical study: *Camberwell School of Arts and Crafts*: its students and teachers, 1943-1960, by Geoff Hassell, published by the Antique Collectors Club, 1995. There are reproductions of Camberwell paintings by: Hilda Briddon, Frank Collins, Eric Doitch, Anthony Eyton, William Lazard, Thomas Monnington, Margaret Whitwell, and Victor Willis.

From an earlier period the catalogues of the Camberwell Public Libraries exhibitions illustrating Camberwell past and present should be noted; items are described and catalogues appeared in 1927, 1933, and 1938.

Lastly, one should note the three collections of loose reproductions (printed in sepia on cream paper), together with notes published by Southwark Libraries in 1974. This *Scenes from the past* series features works from the eighteenth and nineteenth centuries, from many sources, and covers the whole of the borough.

IV: ILLUSTRATED ACCOUNTS OF SPECIFIC ORGANISATIONS OR BUILDINGS

The following, selective listing is arranged alphabetically by name of organisation/building:

BOROUGH MARKET: *An illustrated history of Borough Market*, written by Dominic Webster, Teresa Hoskyns, Jackie Power, and Ray Brown, published in the early 1990's by the Trustees of Borough Market.

BRIDGES: There are three Guildhall Art Gallery catalogues: *London Bridge in art*, 1969; *London Bridge progress drawings* (by E.W. Cooke and Albert Yee), 1975; and *To God and the bridge: the story of the city's bridges in paintings, prints, plans and documents*, 1972. Drawings of London Bridge (old and new) by E.W. Cooke, c. 1830 are also reproduced in publication number 113, 1970 of the London Topographical Society.

GLOBE THEATRE: A recent account is *This wooden 'O': Shakespeare's Globe reborn*, by Barry Day, published by Oberon Books.
June Everett, the Globe's artist in residence has been recording the progress of the Globe since 1980 in wash and line drawings. The centre's newsletter has been replaced recently by a glossy magazine 'Around the Globe'.

GUY'S HOSPITAL: *Guy's Hospital, 1724-1902: a tribute to its founder and a record of its work*, published by Ash & Co in 1903 has a wide range of attractive interior and exterior drawings; there is also an aerial view with a key. Other commemorative surveys have been published by the Guys Hospital Gazette in 1925, 1951, and 1976. In 1954 Longmans published *Mr Guy's Hospital*, by H.C. Cameron. The hospital issues post cards and prints of views by David E. Clark, Albany Wiseman and Hanslip Fletcher (1946-48), and there is an illustrated map published by Elton Municipal Maps. There is also an eight-page illustrated booklet on the chapel.

INNS (Borough High Street area): The work of nineteenth century topographical artists features in *The inns of old Southwark and their associations*, by William Rendle and Philip Norman, published by Longmans in 1888. Work by J.C. Buckler, E. Morant Cox, G.P. Jacomb Hood and Philip Norman amongst others is featured.

NUNHEAD CEMETERY: Well served by the publications put out by Friends of Nunhead Cemetery: *Nunhead Cemetery: an illustrated guide*, 1988 contains fourteen specialist articles, including a guided walk (with map) Jeff Hart. The natural history drawings by Maggie Hart are a special feature. Her drawings also appear in *Nunhead remembered*: a collection of stories, anecdotes and observations from Nunhead Cemetery, edited by Rex Batten, 1995. Five nineteenth century engravings are also reproduced. *Nunhead notables*, and *More Nunhead notables*, by Ron Woollacott are illustrated with the author's very effective portrait drawings.

SOUTHWARK CATHEDRAL: There is considerable illustrated literature on the cathedral. In the nineteenth century publications such as: *The history and antiquities of the parochial church of St Saviour, Southwark*, by Rev. J. Nightingale, published in 1818, with fine engravings by W.G. Moss, and just pre-dating the restoration work. Later, there is *The Priory of St Marie Overie Southwark* by F.T. Dollmann, 1888; and *The history and antiquities of the Collegiate Church of St Saviour*, by Rev. W. Thompson, third edition, 1894, printed and published by Ash & Co, with 36 illustrations (many by H.W. Brewer). The work of a variety of illustrators appears in the different editions, 1931, 1939, and 1946 of Canon T.P. Steven's account, including work by Hanslip Fletcher. Fletcher's illustrations also appear in two articles: *London's hidden cathedral*, Pall Mall Magazine, March 1912; and *The cathedral church of Southwark*, by Arthur Reynolds, The Treasury, June, 1905. An exhibition on the history of the cathedral was staged in 1974, and the catalogue lists 42 items. By way of contrast, the guide book published by the Cathedral and Jarrold Publishing in 1990 has resplendent colour photographs. Its more specialist companion publication is *Stained glass in Southwark cathedral*, by Kenneth London (of Glaziers' Hall), published by the cathedral in 1993.

OTHER COLLECTIONS OF INSPIRED GRAPHIC ART FROM PETER MARCAN PUBLICATIONS

A LONDON DOCKLANDS ALBUM: a collection of nineteenth and twentieth century picture material from diverse sources. Second, revised impression.
ISBN: 1 871811 12 0   68pp.   (125 illustrations).

... "a fascinating collection of pictures. *East London Advertiser.*
... "a must for all collectors of East London memorabilia." *East London Record.*
... "each illustration is carefully captioned, making this much more than a picture book and giving it depth and value to anyone interested in the local history of the area." *Docklands News.*

A BERMONDSEY AND ROTHERHITHE ALBUM: a collection of nineteenth and twentieth century picture material; photographs by Lesley McDonald, historical notes, and descriptive, imaginative writing.
ISBN: 1 871811 06 6   106pp.   (185 illustrations).

... "a book which any lover of local history will find fascinating." *Docklands News.*
... "furnished with passages of very readable and evocative text." *Journal of the London Society.*

AN EAST LONDON ALBUM: a collection of nineteenth and twentieth century picture material from diverse sources relating to the London Boroughs of Tower Hamlets, Hackney, and Newham.
ISBN: 1 871811 07 4   102pp.   (114 illustrations).

... "full of fascinating pictures." *East London Advertiser.*

THE LORD'S PRAYER IN BLACK AND WHITE, WITH DRAWINGS BY ARTHUR WRAGG. First published in 1946, and now re-issued to revive the name and work of a great English visionary graphic artist.
ISBN: 1 871811 01 5   26pp.

... "strikingly original drawings." *Church Times.*
... "the pictures are challenging to a fascinating extent." *Harry Williams, Community of the Resurrection, Mirfield.*
... "a magnificent booklet ... Arthur Wragg's drawings are absolutely superb." *The Right Rev. Dr George Carey.*